PUBLISHING

YOUR ART

AS CARDS, POSTERS & CALENDARS

PUBLISHING
YOUR ART
AS CARDS, POSTERS & CALENDARS

HAROLD DAVIS

The Consultant Press, Ltd.
New York, NY

Publishing Your Art As Cards, Posters & Calendars

Library of Congress Catalog Card Number: 93-29040

ISBN: 0-913069-42-6

Printed and bound in the United States of America.

Cover Photograph: *Rowboat, Sorrento, Maine* © Harold Davis 1987.
Design: Phyllis Davis.
Edited by: Susan P. Levy.

Published by:
The Consultant Press, Ltd.
163 Amsterdam Avenue
New York, NY 10023
212-838-8640

Distributed by:
Career Press
180 Fifth Avenue
Hawthorne, NJ 07507
800-CAREER-1 ◆ Fax: 201-427-2037

Library of Congress Cataloging-in-Publication Data:
Davis, Harold.
      Publishing your art as cards, posters & calendars / by Harold Davis — 2nd ed.
            p.   cm.
      Includes bibliographical references and index.
      ISBN 0-913069-42-6 : $19.95
            1. Greeting cards—Marketing.   2. Posters—Marketing.   3. Calendars—Marketing.
      4. Self-publishing.   I. Title.
      NC1860.D38   1993   741.6'068'8—dc20   93-29040   CIP

10 9 8 7 6 5 4 3 2 1

Second Edition.

This book is dedicated to artists everywhere.

Preface to the Revised Edition

Publishing Your Art As Cards & Posters first appeared in 1990 and has gone through several printings since then. For a number of reasons—both practical and philosophic—a complete revision and extensive expansion of the book has become appropriate. This revision gives me the opportunity to update information that has become dated. I have also been able to incorporate answers to many of the questions raised by readers of the first edition. One respect in which this edition constitutes a major enlargement of the scope of the book is the inclusion of information on the calendar market. This is reflected in the new title: *Publishing Your Art As Cards, Posters & Calendars.*

In the introduction to the first edition of *Publishing Your Art As Cards & Posters* I stated, "... the purpose of this book is to help the artist think like a business person who is creating, marketing and controlling a product." While this remains an admirable goal—and one which I hope the present volume will help support—

readers will find the primary focus of the revised edition to have shifted. This new and expanded version of the book is intended as a definitive manual on the nuts and bolts process of publishing art as cards, posters and calendars. This can be broken down into three connected and overlapping segments. First, there is finding or creating publishable art. Second, there is the science (or art) of design, production and printing. Finally, work must be brought to market. These three steps can never be considered entirely in a vacuum or in the sequential order presented above. For example, market research as to whether a certain style or kind of art can be distributed should often precede the creation or acquisition of that art.

In order to facilitate a more complete and empirical view of the process, material has been added to this book to cover the following areas: the details of production and printing; working with printing and graphics arts vendors; faithful reproduction of artwork; the preparation of mechanicals; desktop publishing and its applications both to the production process and the card and poster market; calendars and the calendar market. Also, I have included a section of color reproductions of fine art posters and cards that are successful in the marketplace.

The first edition of *Publishing Your Art As Cards & Posters* told my story as an artist and how I founded Wilderness Studio as a vehicle for the publication of my own work. Much of the text was based on my experience, and the tone was autobiographical. This edition, on the other hand, contains only a brief section on my experiences with self-publishing and Wilderness Studio in the introductory chapter. It

is sufficient to establish that my credentials to write on the topic have surely been earned the hard way (for which there is no substitute). This revised edition will present a broader and more detailed view of the field with less attention to my career. After all, this book is intended to be useful to you and to provide the information that you need to successfully publish and market your work. I believe that the best way I can do this is by providing detailed, practical, thorough and complete information in as comprehensive a form as possible.

Harold Davis
New York, NY
August, 1993

Contents

List of Diagrams, Illustrations, Reproductions and Sample Documents

1.

Introduction and Overview: Cards, Posters, and Calendars

There is a broad and insufficiently appreciated market for art that is reproducible as a component part of a card, poster or calendar (sometimes referred to by the blanket term "Paper Products market"). This often overlooked market represents one of the fields of greatest opportunity for the independent artist. Success is possible without achieving fame or a critical reputation. Unknown artists, whose works are good and appropriate for this market, may break into it fairly easily and reap substantial financial rewards. Individual pieces of artwork can stand on their own in this market. In contrast, consider the publication of a book of an artist's work, where successful publication requires a cohesive and integrated body of reproductions along with text.

What is this market? How does the paper products industry work? What kinds of imagery and products are successful within it? How does an original work of art—oil painting, watercolor, drawing, collage, photograph, etc.—get turned into a card, poster or other paper product? How does an artist break into this field? What are the pitfalls to be avoided? What steps should be taken to maximize income? These questions, and more, are answered in *Publishing Your Art As Cards, Posters & Calendars*. There is no other single source for this information. The focus of this book is primarily to give information and advice to the artist. It should also be useful to publishers and to those generally interested in the paper products industry.

This chapter starts with a brief summary of my personal experiences in self-publishing and as the founder of Wilderness Studio. The chapter continues with overviews of the different segments of the industry, followed by a synopsis of the reproduction process and an outline of the marketing opportunities for artists. Sufficient background information is presented in this chapter to give a very basic familiarity with the workings of the Paper Products industry. The topics raised in this overview are covered in more depth in the relevant portions of the book.

Throughout the book, special attention is given to areas of opportunity for artists. Every effort is made to describe how the Paper Products industry works and how its workings can benefit individual artists. Potential pitfalls, and things to watch out for, are also noted. The ability to make good art is perhaps innate and certainly not easily taught. But the tools needed to market that art—to see it published and financially rewarded—can and should be learned by every artist.

MY EXPERIENCES SELF-PUBLISHING

The previous edition of *Publishing Your Art As Cards & Posters* included many anecdotes about my experiences founding and running Wilderness Studio, Inc. Specific publication ventures of mine and their successes or failures were discussed. The rationale for this inclusion was that my experiences served an educational purpose.

It is true that there is no teacher like experience. The person who would like to become an entrepreneur—and the artist who would like to self-publish—is best off researching, coming up with a plan, starting a business and getting on with it. This is true even if his first venture fails.

Failure should not be regarded as the end of the world. Those who fear failure to excess will never take the risks needed to succeed.

Failure can also be extremely educational. As one artist told me about her failed print reproduction business, "I'm glad I tried it although we went out of business after four years. I learned more about running a business than I would have by getting an M.B.A., and it cost a lot less."

The key point to realize is that it is the job of your business to support you and enable you to do what you want to in life. If the business becomes a financial and emotional drain over the long term, it is time to change the business as well as the way you operate it. Artists who start self-publishing businesses must take steps to insure that they continue to grow as artists and that they operate their businesses and life intelligently and flexibly. They must remember that making money is not their sole objective. (These issues will be discussed in more detail in Chapter 11, *A More Detailed Look at the Self-Publishing Option.*)

To a great extent it is also true that advice to artists about self-publishing can validly be given only by someone who has, "walked the walk." In this sense, my authority to write *Publishing Your Art As Cards, Posters & Calendars* is primarily based on my hard-won experience as a self-publishing artist. This section will briefly recount the history of Wilderness Studio to keep the record straight and to educate the reader via a true life up and down self-publishing artist success story. It is a statement of some of my qualifications to write this book. Elsewhere in this edition I have dropped the autobiographic approach.

Wilderness Studio was founded in 1978 (the year I graduated from law school) in a loft near Union Square in New York City. The intention behind Wilderness Studio—to the extent that there was an intention at that time—was that it was to be a moneymaking vehicle to support my personal interest in photography of wilderness areas. The Union Square area was then filled with photography studios that specialized in fashion, cosmetics and tabletop work. I asked, "Why not a Wilderness Studio?"

In 1980 I had an exhibition of my original color prints in a 57th Street Gallery in Manhattan. This exhibition started a chain of events that led in two directions. David Lingwood of Modernart Editions published a successful poster of my work to go with the exhibition. I appreciated the idea of combining graphics and good design with my photography. The Modernart Editions poster led to posters published by other publishers and, eventually, to my self-publication of posters under the name Wilderness Studio.

The other direction that the exhibition led to was into cards. *American Photographer* printed a review of my exhibition and reproduced one of my photographs in their magazine. Later, they published the image as a postcard as part of an advertising promotion. They gave me some postcards, and I discovered I could easily sell them to card stores. I began self-publishing first postcards and, later, a line of blank note cards.

By 1983, the year Wilderness Studio incorporated, its main thrust was publishing my work as posters and cards. (I continued to accept photography assignments, to sell original prints and to work with outside publishers.)

Here is the Wilderness Studio card story in brief. There was a partnership followed by a divorce from a major commercial printer. The printer printed and handled the business. I supplied the imagery and received a percentage of the gross. Following the divorce, I took over the business side as well. In its peak year, 1987, Wilderness Studio had over one hundred different styles of blank note cards, a national network of sales "reps," and hundreds of accounts. But it had become clear to me that I had to decide between building a national card business and pursuing my other interests. I chose to let the card business go by attrition, filling orders that came in but not reprinting or soliciting new orders. (In the 1990s this might be called "downsizing.") Today, Wilderness Studio is for all practical purposes out of the card business. (Others, however, have found the card business extremely rewarding.)

Here is the Wilderness Studio poster story in brief. I found posters to be more rewarding than cards. Per-unit profits were higher; they were artistically interesting, and centralized distribution companies removed many business headaches. A number of Wilderness Studio posters of my work turned out to be ongoing industry best-sellers. "The Dance of Spring is the Dance of Life" and "Denali, the Great One, Alaska" are two notable successes. Publication of posters that varied from my usual wilderness landscapes has not been profitable. Therefore, I'm sticking to my original niche of photography of the natural landscape. Wilderness Studio anticipates an ongoing participation as a publisher of my work in the fine art poster industry. It is doing well and enables me to photograph for love, not money.

The point is, the journey matters, not the destination. You never know where the road is going to take you. Approach self-publishing your art with openness and a sense of humor. Don't let it become routine—once it does, the art is gone. It's much better to change and grow, trying all kinds of things and learning all you can, than it is to get caught up in self-referential navel-watching art world twaddle. So much for my philosophy. Now, back to business.

CARDS

Retail sales through card stores or from dedicated sales racks in more general stores, such as supermarkets, variety stores, or bookstores, is the primary method by which the huge volume of greeting cards sold in the United States reach their end-market. ("Rack", or "Rack space", is a retailer's term for shelf or display space in a store.) There is no uniform method of distribution or sales to these stores, presenting a considerable problem to small independent publishers or artists who would like to market their work on their own.

Large card companies have full-time staffs of sales representatives whose jobs are to sell the companies' products to retail stores. It is also the responsibility of these sales representatives to "service the racks". This means that they must see that merchandise displayed is seasonally updated (Christmas from November on, Valentine's Day in January, etc.), that it consists of likely sellers for the store, rack, and neighborhood, and it is not soiled from too much customer handling.

The greeting card industry is dominated by a few large publishers such as Hallmark and American Greetings. While these companies make every effort to update their designs and to make them appealing to consumers, a substantial part of the continued success of these big businesses has to do with "captive rack space" arrangements.

The term "captive rack space" refers to a contractual arrangement between a card publisher and a "captive" retail store where the store is obliged to reserve all (or some high percentage) of its available rack space for product from the publisher. Often, stores operating on this basis will be designated by the card publisher's name, e.g., "Hallmark" store.

While the industry is dominated by its giants, there are also a great quantity—numbering in the thousands—of independent card publishing companies. Many of these are highly successful. Emphasizing their concern with creative design and more contemporary life-style issues, a number of the largest of the independents founded in the late 1970s and early 1980s have become known as "Alternative Card Companies". Recycled Paper Greetings of Chicago is perhaps the best known of the alternative card companies, with sales in the tens of millions annually and its own highly effective sales network.

Stepping down the ladder of size even further, quite a few extremely small "Mom & Pop" card publishers do very well. Generally, small independent card publishers must have a distinctive look and marketing niche. Their product is sold to retail stores by independent card sales representatives (also known as "manufacturer's reps" or "sales reps").

According to industry statistics, over 95% of the cards sold in the United States are "occasion-related". The "occasion" in "occasion-related" could be a holiday, such as Christmas. Christmas cards account for a very substantial portion of annual greeting card sales. (The popularity of holiday-related cards has led to the invention by the card industry of quite a number of now popularly accepted holidays.)

The occasion could also be personal, for example, "Happy Birthday". Birthday cards are second in sales only to Christmas cards. Birthdays and seasonal holidays comprise the principal subject matter of salable card designs. In addition, with the rise of the alternative card companies, a somewhat new kind of card has appeared. This is the "message" card. "I miss you," is one message; "I'm sorry I wasn't sensitive to your feelings," is another.

Almost without exception the art for all cards—whether the card is for a seasonal occasion, a personal occasion, or delivers a message—falls into two categories: traditional and humorous. An example of the traditional is a Christmas card depicting a snowy New England village, or Santa on a sleigh. Humorous cards often depict a cartoon character and deliver a surprise punch line once they are opened. Within the broad categories of "traditional" and "humorous", there is tremendous variation in the subject matter of the art utilized. Media of art that is published also ranges widely, from watercolor and oil painting to collage, photography and computer-generated art.

It is perhaps obvious, but should nevertheless be stated, that card art does not stand alone without words. One of the most important tasks of the successful card designer is to effect a marriage between the visual art and the text to create a complete card.

The greeting card industry has an immense need for art. This is a need that is never satiated because of the industry's constant need for fresh and novel product. The market for greeting card art will always be open to talented newcomers as well as seasoned professionals. It is a market that can use work in every media and in a great variety of genres.

POSTERS

There are two almost completely distinct poster industries. The first involves imagery, often of rock and roll stars, celebrities, or other trendy material, that will go in teenagers' rooms or in similar casual settings, usually unframed. Generally, the retail price for this kind of poster will be less than $10.00. Distribution mechanisms are much the same as those used for greeting cards, with variety chain stores such as K-Mart and record stores serving as important vehicles for retail sales. With perfect timing and intimate knowledge of current pop culture, it is certainly possible to be successful with this kind of poster. However, longevity of sales is probably out of the question. Also, to take advantage of pop trends (Ninja Turtles, pet rocks, David Bowie, whatever) distribution must be substantially in place long before the product is created. And substantial licensing fees will have to be paid to the owner of the pop phenomenon.

Of far more importance to the artist, for a variety of reasons, is the fine art poster.

This poster is intended to go on walls, generally framed, as an art object. The retail price of an art poster (unframed) ranges upwards from $25.00. Channels of distribution for this kind of poster diverge widely from the system in the greeting card industry. The nature of the fine art poster business has led to *de facto* centralization of distribution which can work to greatly benefit the individual artist or small publisher.

Historically, the fine art poster was derived from three sources: art deco and art nouveau advertising posters; photo-mechanical reproductions of classical paintings; and exhibition posters which were designed to promote an artist's show at a gallery or museum. This century has seen a tremendous increase in the price of art. First paintings, and then, by the late 1970s, original prints such as lithographs and etchings grew too expensive for many institutional decor uses and for purchase as an everyday affair by the middle class. In the early 1980s the fine art poster industry, under innovative leaders such as David Lingwood of Modernart Editions, expanded to fill this void with quality art, both contemporary and historical, reproduced photo-mechanically, and sold at an affordable retail price. Generally, the frame is more expensive than the poster. While the retail price of the poster itself ranges from $25.00 to $50.00, once it has been handsomely framed, it becomes a $75.00 to $200.00 item.

Unlike cards, where use implies disposal by the consumer (e.g. they are mailed once), posters are intended to have some degree of longevity. What this means is that a consumer will buy only a certain quantity of posters, generally limited by available wall space. (There is a positive correlation between poster sales and new construction starts.) And, no one poster purchaser is ever very likely to buy more than one or two of any given poster. This leads to a marketplace that can be characterized as rather shallow but very broad, meaning that there are very many possible purchasers of posters (limited only by available wall space), but most purchasers will not buy in great quantity or in multiples of a single stock item.

In addition to consumers who purchase fine art posters for their homes, institutional sales are extremely important to this market. Fine art posters end up in offices, back offices, and public areas in businesses, hospitals and hotels.

Approximately ten large companies currently control the distribution of fine art posters in the United States. The largest of these companies, each with a slightly different slant, are Bruce McGaw Graphics, Graphique de France, and the New York Graphic Society. All of the distribution companies also function as publishers (some, such as New York Graphic, regard this as their primary and almost exclusive orientation), meaning that in addition to buying already printed posters from independent artists and publishers for resale, they also work directly with artists on a royalty basis to create their own product.

A number of artists make very good livings completely, or almost completely, on the basis of art poster sales of their works. But beyond financial reward, what makes this a particularly attractive area is its potential as a showcase. By its very nature, the art poster is a medium which says that its imagery is worthy of consideration as art.

CALENDARS

There are two basic forms of illustrated calendars: monthly hanging wall calendars with twelve images; and desk engagement calendars with weekly or bi-weekly illustrations, generally spiral bound. Each type of calendar will have a cover image, which is usually a repetition of one of the images from inside the calendar.

The primary mode of distribution of calendars is via the book trade, with bookstores being the most important retail outlet. A secondary, but still significant, distribution method is to sell via sales "repping" organizations to card and variety stores.

Also of note to the artist, but completely different in intention and orientation, are the calendars which are not marketed to consumers at all, but are instead given away as corporate gifts. This is a very prestigious and lucrative business in some parts of the world, particularly Japan.

It is extremely difficult for an independent publisher to break into the consumer calendar market. Because of the seasonal and dated nature of the materials, publishers have only one short time period in which to sell their merchandise to this market. Calendar sales to retail outlets for a given year generally take place from March through September of the previous year. For example, all sales to stores of 1995 calendars will have to be completed by September of 1994. Any remaining merchandise after that point is worthless. This means that calendars must be planned far in advance and with precision timing of production. Also, neither book distributors nor card sales "repping" organizations, with very rare exceptions, will take on a company that produces only one or two calendars.

Fundamentally, the artist who wishes to break into this market is best off by licensing work to the existing large calendar publishers. There are two ways to do this. One is on an image-by-image basis in response to the request lists that are sent to artists several years in advance of calendar production for a particular year. Since calendars are based on a theme, the other possibility is for an artist with some design skills to put together a mock-up of a calendar of his work based on an imaginative, effective and appropriate theme. This calendar can then be licensed in its entirety to a publisher.

THE REPRODUCTION PROCESS

Cards, posters and calendars are, almost without exception, reproduced via the offset process. (Certain products, particularly in the card industry, are embellished with special effects such as embossing, die-cutting and metallic stamping subsequent to offset printing.)

The term "offset" is short for "offset lithographic printing". In this process, developed in the early part of this century, a high speed sheet-fed printing press offsets ink from a metal plate to a rubber blanket and then to the paper. Sheet-fed presses can print from one to eight colors on a pass of paper through the press, with six being standard for modern equipment. "Spot" or "process" colors are applied by each ink unit on the press. Spot color replicates the actual color of ink used on the finished piece. Process color is a system used for reproducing the full range of perceived color by breaking art down into its component primary colors and recreating these on the press using the three primary colors and black. Many printing jobs combine spot and process colors.

To start the printing process two things must be prepared: a mechanical, and the art. Essentially, a mechanical is a map and guide for the printer of how the printing process will proceed. The mechanical also usually includes "line art", for example typography and lines around a reproduced piece.

As should be clear from this brief introductory discussion, printing technology is quite complex and expensive. Any publisher, and any artist who wishes to have his art published in this market, must understand at least the basics of the process. Chapter 3, *The Print Reproduction Process from A to Z*, will cover it in greater depth.

MARKETING OPPORTUNITIES

The paper products industry presents a very considerable opportunity for accomplished, business-like creators of art.

The chaotic distribution practices of the greeting card industry, combined with its constant need for fresh material, keep many free-lancers busy. In addition, artists with work having a unique look or viewpoint (if they are willing to take the risks of an entrepeneur and devote time to business management issues and to selling) may be able to create their own highly profitable long-term business.

Centralized distribution of the fine art poster industry creates two kinds of opportunities in this highly profitable arena where the product itself is a prestige showcase for the artist's work. Poster publishers are constantly searching for artwork available for licensing which will sell well in this market. And self-starters can publish their own posters which can be sold into the existing distribution network obviating the need for creating a substantial business organization or doing any

selling other than the most rudimentary selling. If their posters do well, they can reap substantial financial rewards commensurate with the risks they have taken.

Artists who have created appropriate imagery have a good chance of licensing it for future use by a calendar publisher. If the artist can put together a thematically strong and graphically effective complete calendar, it is also licensable as a package to publishers.

While there are many opportunities for artists in the Paper Products industry, it is a complex and little understood field. To be successful in it, artists must be knowledgable about the needs and realities of this business. They must also be prepared to behave in an appropriate, business-like and professional manner. *Publishing Your Art As Cards, Posters & Calendars* guides the reader through this maze, starting with chapters on selecting imagery that works, the print reproduction process, creating designs, and working with printers. Next, there is an in-depth look at each of the separate markets involved: cards, posters and calendars. The book concludes with a detailed look at the pluses and minuses of self-publication followed by answers to the questions most commonly asked by those trying to get their work published. I hope that the information in this book serves your needs whether you are a beginner or a seasoned professional artist. I wish you luck in your publication endeavors. ◆

2.

Imagery that Works

The president of a major fine art poster publishing and distributing company notes, "We publish ten posters. Five make money; two lose money; three break even. We never really know which will be which. We publish enough volume that in these ratios we make money in the long run." While this statement is an exaggeration—publishers who remain in business are very good at choosing successful art for their products—it illuminates something essential to understand about image selection in the Paper Products industry; whatever the experts say, no one really knows for sure which design will work until the consumers have spoken. The point of this is not that there are no general guidelines regarding imagery that works as cards, posters and calendars. There are, and they will be discussed later. The bottom line is that the experts can be wrong. Standard guidelines can be faulty. There have been and will continue to be eccentric and unconventional paper product winners. (Unfortunately, there have also been "sure thing" losers.) This is an industry dominated by personal taste, and taste is a subjective and changing matter. To get your work published successfully, you may be required to put your own money where your art is and back your art (your taste) when no one else will do so.

HOW TO CREATE IT

There is no magic formula for creating art that will be successful. I believe that as your primary goal you should choose to create work that satisfies you. If you consciously choose to create work that will sell as a primary goal, you will probably fail in the long or short run. It also will not work to attempt to please some particular audience rather than yourself. To create your best work, do not think about its marketability while you are creating it.

In the first edition of this book I called

this principle of dividing functions "Different Hats", and went so far as to suggest assuming different names for the different functions. For example, Harold Davis is an artist; Julian Sorel is his Director of Art Marketing, and Bruce Savage is his bill collector. In reality, they are one; all of them are me.

If this piece of incipient schizophrenia proves useful to you, wear the different hats, and if it does not, don't. But, in any case, do not let the real world interfere too much in your creation of art. Outside, storms may rage. Money to pay the rent and heat the house and feed the baby may be scarce. You may have to work at odd and horrible jobs to continue being an artist. But as long as you are an artist, respect what you create as an artist. Cherish it, protect it, give it space and freedom and privacy, and let your creation of art be a world unto itself. Divorce creating art from marketing art.

Do not look down on yourself or your work if it ultimately is used in a commercial or clichéd way. Many great artists did "commercial" work in their time. And cliches are clichés because they have a grain of universal truth or greatness within them. Otherwise, there would be no general response to the cliché.

Love the work you create and the process of creating it. Be obsessed with it. This is the only reason for being an artist. Work hard at it. Push yourself to your limits and beyond. Technique is important. Learn your craft as best you can: from your own experience; from gifted teachers; from books; from other artists. Leave no stone unturned in your desire to be a better artist. Successful artists are not lazy. Don't be afraid to take risks and experiment, but be a strict editor of your work. Release only the really good work to the world.

Use your art to play. Use it to discover more about your world and yourself. Emulate work you admire. There never has been and never will be a substitute for true quality. When you achieve it, it will be instantly recognizable in your work.

Work in every imaginable medium and style has been successfully used in the Paper Products industry. So here, too, what you must do is be true to yourself. Don't start doing, let's say, nautical watercolors, because they are the trend of the month in the fine art poster world. On the other hand, don't go to the other extreme, either. Don't be afraid to work in new media, and don't refuse to do something just because it has been suggested to you by a publisher.

HOW TO KNOW IT WHEN YOU SEE IT

Cards

There is no substitute for experience. The

best way to learn which imagery works is to review thousands of images over the course of a number of years, getting feedback on which have succeeded and which have not. This experience can be simulated through careful study. Examine work that has succeeded by looking carefully through poster catalogs, card racks in better stores, and the calendar inventory of good bookstores in retail calendar season (October through December). Open a dialogue (and try to listen more than talk) with owners and salespeople in graphics galleries, frame shops, and card stores. Read relevant trade publications such as *Art Business News*, *Decor*, *Greetings Magazine*, and *Publishers Weekly*.

Card images can consist entirely of pure calligraphy. Or they can be nature photographs with no words at all. They can be cut out roller coasters with slots for the roller coaster structure and watercolor renderings of the cars and passengers. Whatever the form of the card—and there is an almost limitless range of possibilities—successful card art can be recognized because it incorporates one (or more) of the following:

(1) Conveys a message related to one of the major holidays or personal occasions;

(2) Touches or moves people in a universal (generally positive) way;

(3) Conveys positive feelings about the sender of the card;

(4) Is humorous.

Most successful cards combine two or three of these characteristics.

The first characteristic—conveying a message—is the easiest to pinpoint further. As briefly touched on in the previous chapter, Christmas is the most important holiday to the greeting card industry. Christmas imagery, whether traditional or innovative, is always in demand. But other holidays are also important. These include Easter, Father's Day, Hanukkah, Mother's Day, Passover and Valentine's Day, not to mention such synthetic holidays as Secretary's Day. Art that in some way connotes resurrection might be appropriate for an Easter card. So might a watercolor of a bunny rabbit. Art that portrays kind fathers or traditionally male objects (fishing rods, slippers and pipe by the blazing hearth) might work on a Father's Day card. An image of a menorah, possibly abstracted, is a possibility for a Hanukkah card. And so on.

We have noted that the most important personal occasion message for the card industry is "Happy Birthday". There are many ways to say "Happy Birthday" in pictures, ranging from the respectful and affectionate to the humorous and frankly nasty. Any image that manages to portray time passing without also implying that the recipient is getting older will probably do very well as a birthday card.

In terms of volume of cards sold, the next most important personal occasion cards (after birthday greetings) are the romantic card, followed by the congratulatory card, and then the condolence card. Imagery that is either warm and sumptuous or humorous and playful is likely to work best for the romantic message card. Anything that relates to hearts is a good bet. The beautiful still life of flowers can work, as can abstracts.

There are a number of subdivisions within the congratulatory card category, for example, graduation or promotion. Imagery for these cards tends to be representational in a stylized fashion and topical: a graduation cap and gown.

The condolence card tends to have the most insipid and cliched art in the genre, for example, third-rate florals. This is because of the tendency to be very timid around death. No one wants to take the chance of offending with a condolence card.

Finally, there are also miscellaneous messages that have to do with the stresses and relationships of modern living. These cards are often referred to as "Alternative" or "New Age". Examples include "divorce" cards (a card that is in dubious taste at best) and cards that articulate feelings that are difficult for the sender to express on his own. With this kind of message card, imagery must be tailored very closely to the text of the card.

Almost at the other end of the spectrum from Alternative Cards are cards that touch or move people in a deep and universal way. Although sometimes these cards employ text or poetry, very often

they are blanks (meaning they have no text inside). Often—although not universally—the imagery consists of a reproduction of the work of an acknowledged master such as Ansel Adams or Renoir or Rothko.

More than with any other kind of card, these cards are usually after-thoughts to the creation of the art. The artist creates his deeply moving imagery for his own reasons. Someone else comes along and wonders, "Wouldn't that make a great card?"

However, just as moral decisions in real life are never totally black or white, greeting cards are never totally what they seem. The occasion or message card with an image with a whiff of greatness will appeal (perhaps unconsciously) to many more people than an entirely mundane card.

This ties into the third characteristic of the successful card. A card represents the sender. Its quality reflects on him. Production values are particularly important here, which is why one sees so many cards that employ fancy finishing techniques such as embossing, dye cutting and laminating. By choosing the artwork used on the card, the consumer is stating, "This is my taste. It is who I am. I have chosen it for you. You are worth it." If a member of the buying public can identify with the art, and feel represented by it in a positive way, probably the card will be successful.

The fourth characteristic, humor, is a

two-edged sword. On the one hand, many "humorous" greeting cards have a subtext of aggression and hostility. For example, consider all the "funny" birthday cards supposedly advising the recipients not to worry about being older all the while hammering in the fact of advancing age. On the other hand, many cards are genuinely humorous in a good-natured and quirky way. Much of the work of Gary Larson and Boynton falls into this category. Artistic cards with a genuine, caring and original sense of humor sell very well.

One other kind of card—which might be considered humorous or might be thought to fill its own category—is designed for special interest constituencies. Examples include: raunchy, explicit sex cards; Star Trek cards; and fantasy cards. Obviously, cards with specialized themes require unusual methods of distribution, which is naturally more limited than with cards of general interest. However, some companies that specialize in these niches do quite well. They need artists who are familiar with the vagaries of their particular genre. If you know "Hamlet in the original Klingon" you may find a ready market for your work within a specialty niche.

Posters

Successful poster imagery is closest to the second category of card art, that which is genuinely moving, in and of itself. Ansel Adams and Monet are two of the best selling poster artists.

The broadest categories of poster art are abstractions, still lifes and landscapes. Since people frame art posters and place them on their walls, the image must have the ability to be looked at many times without growing stale. Since many posters are purchased for office or institutional environments, the imagery must be relaxing. If the image is a landscape—and photography is a very successful media for landscape art posters—then the place depicted should be one where the purchaser would like to be or for which has nostalgic fondness.

Most posters combine words with their imagery. Successful posters are well-designed indeed. But the delivery of a message on the part of the art is not important the way it is with greeting card art. The image reproduced on the art poster stands essentially alone. It is the poster.

Successful poster art can primarily be recognized by its:

(1) Quality;

(2) Broad appeal;

(3) Workability in a wide variety of interior decor schemes.

Calendars

In general, calendar art can be thought of as somewhere in between card art and poster art. It has neither the disposability of the card nor the longevity of the art poster. The calendar's size is intermediate between the two other forms. If it goes on the wall, it does so in a comparatively modest way with the statement, "I am a useful object," rather than, "I am an art object."

Photography, and, in particular, nature photography, works particularly well in calendars. (The Sierra Club calendars are always popular.) Almost any art is the potential subject matter for a calendar provided that it is:

(1) Generally upbeat;

(2) A cohesive, related and connected body of imagery;

(3) Of substantial interest to at least some people.

Of course, this discussion on recognizing successful imagery has only touched the most basic issues involved. Across the spectrum of the Paper Products industry, no work of art is complete in and of itself. Art must be designed, printed and distributed. The next three chapters of *Publishing Your Art As Cards, Posters & Calendars* discuss the details of the reproduction process. Subsequent chapters discuss, in depth, marketing art, either to existing publishers or as completed products. ◆

3.

The Printing Reproduction Process from A to Z

STEP-BY-STEP GUIDE TO THE OFFSET REPRODUCTION PROCESS

As mentioned in passing in the Introduction, the vast bulk of paper products have been published using the photo offset lithography process. This process may be referred to as "offset lithography" or, more simply, "offset". In general usage, when one states that one is going to "get something printed", it is probably the offset process that is being referenced. In general terms, the following steps (which will each be examined in more detail either in this or subsequent chapters) are involved in reproducing artwork via offset. (Note that in this summary the term "publisher" is used to mean "the printer's client", for example, an artist self-publishing work, or an art poster publishing company.)

(1) A mechanical is created, and the art is prepared for reproduction. See Chapter 4, *Creating a Design for Publication* for instructions on how to do this.

(2) Written specifications for the printing job are prepared on the basis of the mechanical, the finishing and packing desired, and the quantity of the finished piece required. Estimates are solicited from printers on the basis of the specifications. A printer is selected by the publisher on the basis of the quotation and other factors such as demonstrated quality of previous work. Chapter 5, *Dealing with Printers and Other Graphic Arts Professionals* discusses these topics in depth.

(3) Separations are created using laser scanners for 4-color portions of the printing job. A transparency or print of the artwork is placed on a scanning drum which passes light through or onto the art. The results are fed into a computer which uses sophisticated programs to separate the image into its four component "process" colors. The computer generates a piece of film for each of these process colors. Since offset printing is a

Flow Chart of the Print Reproduction Process

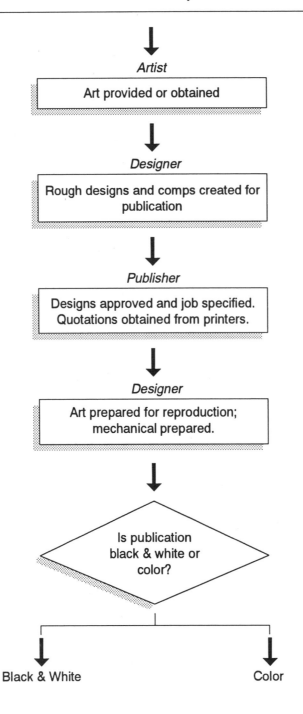

Artist

Art provided or obtained

Designer

Rough designs and comps created for publication

Publisher

Designs approved and job specified. Quotations obtained from printers.

Designer

Art prepared for reproduction; mechanical prepared.

Is publication black & white or color?

Black & White

Color

(Continued on the top of the next page.)

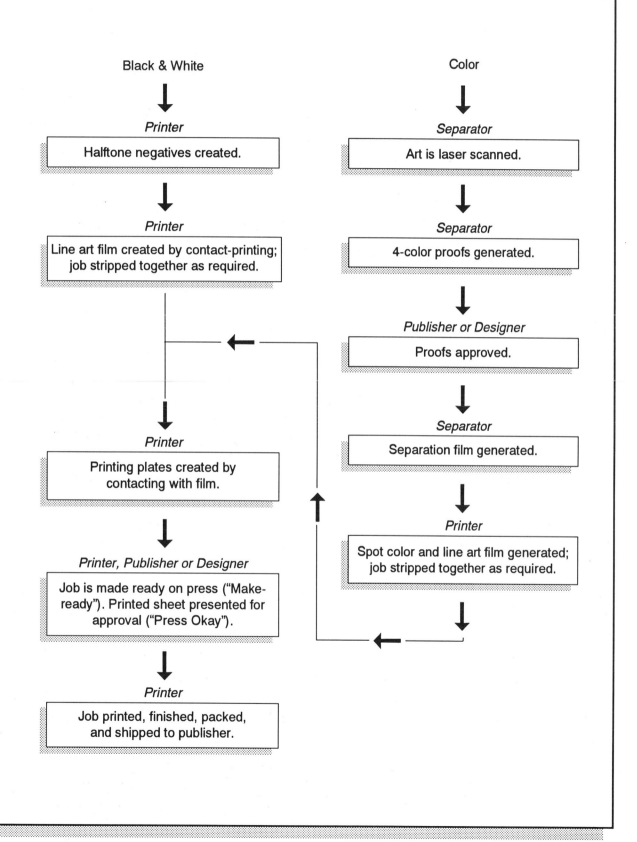

Black & White

↓

Printer

Halftone negatives created.

↓

Printer

Line art film created by contact-printing; job stripped together as required.

↓

Printer

Printing plates created by contacting with film.

↓

Printer, Publisher or Designer

Job is made ready on press ("Make-ready"). Printed sheet presented for approval ("Press Okay").

↓

Printer

Job printed, finished, packed, and shipped to publisher.

Color

↓

Separator

Art is laser scanned.

↓

Separator

4-color proofs generated.

↓

Publisher or Designer

Proofs approved.

↓

Separator

Separation film generated.

↓

Printer

Spot color and line art film generated; job stripped together as required.

↓

process that uses dots for reproductions (generally smaller in size than can be seen by the naked eye), separation film is "screened" into a dot pattern. These dots are called "halftones". The color separation halftone films are called "separations" for short.

(4) "Proofs" of the separations are created from the film. These proofs, which are intended to give an early idea of what the 4-color elements of the final printed piece will look like once the four pieces of film have been contacted to make printing plates and re-combined on press, are reviewed and corrected or approved by the publisher. If corrections are major, the computer generates new film and proofs based on them.

(5) Film is generated for non-process (see the next section of this chapter for discussion of the distinction between process and non-process color) elements of the job. A different piece of film must be created for each item of non-process art or other element that will appear in the final printed piece. Generally, this is done by photographing or contact printing typography or spot color art that has been prepared by the designer or production artist.

(6) The various elements of the job are composed together. This means that film is created in the final form for plate-making with one piece of film for each color that will be printed with everything—4-color imagery, typography, spot color, varnishes, registration marks and trim

lines—properly configured. If the publisher is combining a number of small sized items together so that they will fit on a larger printing sheet—as will usually be the case when greeting cards are produced—this is the step in which the individual pieces are joined and a "flat" is created. Composition can be done on the computer or by skilled employees of the printer or pre-press shop using "stripping" (physically joining pieces of film) and contact printing on vacuum tables. Composed film is carefully examined for holes—which, should they not be noticed, will print as solid dots or lines of color. If holes are found, they are painted out using special opaque lithographer's ink.

(7) A monochromatic proof is generated by combining the composed film so the publisher can make sure that all elements have been positioned correctly. Generally, this proof is created using an inexpensive cyanotype contacting process and is called a "blue line". It is the publisher's last chance to check for placement and typographic errors.

(8) A separate printing plate for each "color" that is to print is created by contact-printing the composed film with a photo-sensitive printing plate. (Note that the term "color" as used in the reproduction process includes not only process and spot colors but also any varnishes or finishes that are applied on press.)

(9) The job is printed. Generally, cards, posters and calendars are printed on sheet-

fed presses with from one to eight color units. Each color unit prints one color by transferring the image from the inked plate to a rubber blanket. The blanket, not the plate, is placed in contact with the paper and actually prints the image. The term "offset" is used to describe this entire printing process because the image is offset from plate to blanket and blanket to paper. Offset printing produces a sharper image than direct plate to paper printing because the blanket conforms to surface variations in the paper. Also, offset plates are easy to work with because they are "right reading"—the plate reads with the same orientation as the final product. (If the image went directly from plate to paper, the plate would have to be backwards; it could be correctly viewed with a mirror.)

Further discussion of the actual printing process, and what to expect when the publisher stands by and approves a product as adjustments are being made to the printing press, will be found in the "Go-ing On Press" (the term used for this experience in the trade) section of Chapter 5.

(10) The printed sheets are allowed to dry. Once dry, they are passed through the printing press again, if necessary, for printing on the back, for adding additional colors, for spot varnishing, or for any other reason.

(11) The dry sheets are finished. If the job calls for it, they are burnished, laminated or embossed. They are trimmed to exact size and, if necessary, cut apart into component units, scored and folded.

(12) Finally, the finished job is packed to specifications and shipped to the publisher.

SEPARATIONS AND SPOT COLOR

The idea of the 4-color process separation is one of the most important—and difficult—concepts related to offset lithography. However, it is imperative to understand it, its strengths and limitations, and

© Harold Davis 1993.

An aluminum printing plate being processed. (All photographs of the printing process in this chapter courtesy CR Waldman.)

how it differs from spot (non-process) color.

The theory of process color is related to the distributive law of algebra and pointillism in painting. How is the color in an artwork to be reproduced? It is, as a practical matter, impossible to duplicate each shade and hue of color with an ink mixed to exactly match that shade and hue simply because the number of different inks required is too many. According to basic principles of color theory, any perceived color can be replaced with its primary-color components, which, when re-combined, will appear to be the original color. We are applying a kind of distributive law—breaking complex colors down into component primaries and re-combining accurately. It is also analogous to pointillism, which is a process, like offset printing, that allows the human eye to get the impression of an overall hue based on combining different colored dots. Another analogy is that of a choir performing a musical score. The audience hears a blending whole, not the component alto, soprano, tenor and bass notes.

The process color model that is generally used for offset separates art into cyan, magenta, yellow and black components. Cyan appears as a kind of blue and magenta as a kind of purple. This is known as the "CMYK" color model ("K" is a printer's abbreviation for black). CMYK separations are neither the only nor the most intuitively obvious separation models. For example, computer monitors and televisions generally use RGB separations, where colors have been separated into red, green and blue components.

In real life, as opposed to theory, there are times when process color either cannot reproduce a perceived color or will not reproduce it well. When this happens, ink is mixed to the exact shade and hue desired (referred to as a "spot" color), and film and a printing plate are created strictly for the spot color.

The major drawback to using a spot color is the additional expense it entails. Each additional color used requires special ink mixing, one more plate and color unit, and perhaps additional passes through the

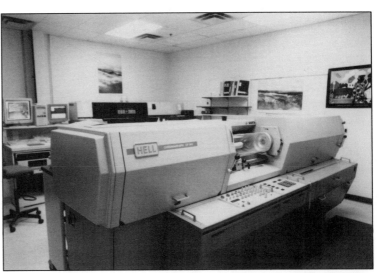

A laser scanner.

© Harold Davis 1993.

printing press. However, many printing jobs require the use of at least some spot color.

Each spot color that is to be used must be specified in a way that printers understand and that provides a framework for communication among artists, publishers and printers. There are a number of color specification systems, but the most commonly used is the Pantone Match System, known as "PMS" color. Pantone supplies ink to printers and sells swatch books to designers containing thousands of graduated and labeled ink choices. Any competent printer can easily and accurately re-create any color specified out of a PMS book. Recently, Pantone has added (very groovy!) metallic inks and a metallic selection swatch book to its line.

Some examples of situations in which spot PMS colors are used instead of or in addition to process color are briefly mentioned here to help the reader achieve a better sense of when spot PMS colors should be speci-

fied. Silver, gold or bronze that has been achieved by foiling or gilding or with enamel in the original artwork will never reproduce well in 4-color process. The edges of 4-color objects can appear fuzzy, so typography reproduced against a white or light background should often be specified as a PMS color. The dots in the screen of backgrounds such as light grey will probably be obvious in 4-color, so solid backgrounds should often be specified as a spot color. And sometimes artwork will have been created with a relatively limited color palate with solely spot reproduction in mind.

Discussion of how to best work with a separator to achieve the results you desire appears in the section on "Getting Good Color Separations" in Chapter 5.

PRE-PRESS

The pre-press process is the step where all the pieces of the printing job are combined and checked. If everything is okay, printing plates will be created.

Modern offset presses use paper that is quite wide. 28"X40" is a

A flat being stripped together.

fairly typical sheet size. This means that, to use the sheet efficiently, a number of smaller items, such as cards, must be combined to print on one "flat" (a printed sheet). The designer must think out how this is to be done carefully, perhaps after consultation with the printer. The designer's mechanical showing this must be accurate and understandable. (See Chapter 4, *Creating a Design for Publication*, for further discussion of the designer's job.)

Another potential problem that must be checked at this stage involves reviewing what is known as "imposition". The imposition is the arrangement of different items and pages in proper sequence as specified in the mechanical. Imposition is reviewed to verify that the right back will be reproduced with its correct front following printing and finishing. Imposition arrangements are most complex with books and calendars. Since cards have printing on the front and back and are arranged in multiples on flats, proper imposition is something of an issue. Once the sheet has gone through the press, it must dry and then be turned over and put back through the press for the printing on the second side. Careful planning on the part of

designers and printers is called for to correctly combine items with front and back printing. Imposition is usually not a cause for concern with art posters because they are printed on only one side of the sheet of paper "one-up" (meaning that the poster is the only item being printed on that sheet).

Pre-press work is extremely important to the overall quality of the job. Checking proofs provided by the printer at the pre-press stage is the publisher's last chance to catch errors—whether made by publisher, designer or printer—before correction becomes extremely expensive.

PRINTING

For an artist or publisher, the experience of attending a press run is both thrilling and terrifying. The press floor of a printing shop is noisy with huge pieces of machinery. It is also chemical-laden. Aes-

Example of a flat.

thetic decisions must be made in this environment. There is additional pressure because the hourly cost of running a press is staggering. Discussion of what to expect when going "On Press" and how best to handle the responsibility will be found in Chapter 5.

A multi-color sheetfed offset printing press is a huge piece of equipment weighing many tons. The press has the approximate dimensions of a tractor trailer. Proper installation of the press requires sophisticated ventilation devices, heavy-duty industrial power, and a multi-level reinforced pit-like structure for the press itself.

Paper is brought to the press on "palettes", wooden platforms used for transporting heavy objects, using a fork lift. The palette is transferred to the press, which hydraulically raises it as paper is used so that the level of the top-most sheet in the feed remains constant.

The sheet of paper is passed through each of the color units on the press. As de-

scribed above, each color unit offsets ink in one color from the printing plate to the blanket to the sheet of paper. After the sheet has passed through all the units, it is gathered on another hydraulically supported palette at the front of the press.

Generally, there will be a viewing station close to the front of the press. The viewing station should be illuminated with accurately balanced light. Sheets are viewed and corrected here as they come out of the press. Modern press rooms have viewing stations equipped with digital color analyzers and computer controls on the ink flow in each color unit. Once a job is printing correctly, the settings of these controls are recorded so that the job can be exactly replicated at a future date.

It is extremely important to understand the volume limitations of the offset process. The "make-ready", which is the process of getting the job right on press, takes between 500 and 1000 sheets of paper. The first finished sheet does not print until after the make-ready. When publishers or printers purchase paper for a job, they must allow extra sheets to cover the needs of the make-ready. Since the cost of the make-ready must be amortized over the rest of the printing job, the

© Harold Davis 1993.

A six-color sheet fed printing press.

per unit cost will be absurdly high on offset runs of fewer than about 2,500 units. Do not expect to print fewer than 2,000 sheets on any offset job. Since the makeready cost, and other fixed one-time expenses, such as the costs of separations, are amortized over the entire print run, offset gets more and more economical as quantities rise and truly comes into its own at about 10,000 copies. (At the other end of the scale, sheet-fed offset presses are generally not used for runs of over 100,000 units. High volume publications—such as mass-circulation magazines—are generally printed on a web press, which prints at a higher speed than sheet-fed presses on an uncut roll of paper.)

BINDING AND FINISHING

The terms "binding" and "finishing" are used to describe everything that happens after the printed sheet comes off the press. For elaborate jobs, this includes applying laminates or other special coatings and die-cutting. But even simple jobs must be trimmed to size. Greeting cards must be scored and folded. Calendars must be bound in some fashion. Afterwards every job must be

packed for shipment to the publisher.

This last step may sound very basic, but it is extremely important. Packing should be discussed and specified with the printer before a job is estimated or started. Many printing jobs have been ruined because of poor packaging. It does you no good to have a job printed perfectly only to have the product ruined on its way to you because of sloppy or careless packaging.

Generally, cards will either be loose-packed in sturdy cartons, or shrink wrapped in dozens and then placed in cartons. Posters are usually packaged in units of one hundred for storage by the publisher. They should be wrapped in kraft paper and placed in sturdy individual cartons of precisely the right dimensions for the block of one hundred posters. Calendars are treated much like books, that is, bulk packed in sturdy cartons containing fifty to one hundred units. Sometimes calendars are individually shrink wrapped.

The finished, packaged product should

Side view of a printing press, showing individual color units.

© Harold Davis 1993.

be placed on palettes and shrink wrapped overall for shipment by common carrier. It is <u>never</u> acceptable for the printer to simply place unpackaged finished product on a palette. Some printers will actually do this even though it leads to the inevitable ruin of the product before it is received by the publisher.

REPRODUCING PHOTOGRAPHY (COLOR AND BLACK & WHITE)

Color

As will be further discussed in the section of Chapter 4 on "Preparing Art for Reproduction", the first step in reproducing any artwork is to get a good photograph of it. This step is usually unnecessary when the original artwork is itself a color photograph. An original transparency (also known by the terms "chrome", "color positive" and, most commonly, "slide") can be scanned directly for separation, and is in some respects, the best possible reproduction source. There is no "loss of a generation" of sharpness and detail (as is the case when you photograph a painting and then reproduce it by scanning the resulting color transparency).

However, it is sometimes desirable to make a "reproduction duplicate" from the original transparency. This is done photographically using film and an enlarger. Reproduction duplicates should be 4"X5" or larger. Reasons for creating a reproduction duplicate include the greater safety provided by doing separation and pre-press work on a copy rather than the original and the ability to color correct and re-touch in the duplicating process. The primary reasons for not using a reproduction duplicate are that it is now one generation removed from the original (just like the photograph of the painting) and the expense. Each high quality reproduction duplicate costs from $50 to $100. This is a small portion of the budget of a project with one image that is to be greatly enlarged such as a poster. But it may be prohibitive for a project involving many originals such as a flat of cards.

Reproduction can also

Finished printed material on palettes waiting for shipment.

Reflected art being placed on the drum of a scanner.

methods, a process camera together with a "line screen" is used to create a halftone negative from the continuous tone photographic print. The line screen is a piece of film that, when contact printed with the photograph of the original, turns the continuous tones of a photographic print to dots ("halftones"). Printing plates are then made from the halftone negatives.

A single halftone reproduction (the least expensive and least satisfactory process) involves making the only printing plate that will be used from one line-screened halftone. A "duotone" reproduction entails making plates from two line-screened halftones and printing them in "register" (exactly aligned). The two plates could both be black ("double dot printing"),

be easily achieved by scanning color prints made from color negative films such as Kodacolor or Fujicolor. This will work best if the print is unmounted, 11"X14" or less (so that it will easily fit on the scanning drum) and is crisp, sharp and not printed on textured paper.

Black & White

There are a number of ways to reproduce black & white photography. All start with a print. It is best if the print is medium glossy with good shadow detail. Prints must be clean and in focus with rich blacks.

Using the traditional

A scanner with reflected art on the drum, with the image to be scanned appearing on the monitor in the upper left.

black and another color such as sepia (giving the appearance of a toned print), or two distinct colors. "Fake duotone printing" is the placement of a solid tint of color beneath a line-screened halftone which will print in black. It is termed "fake" because one of the apparent halftone printing passes has actually been created with a solid block of color (not screened with dots). True duotone, with two actual halftone plates, is more pleasing (and more expensive) than fake duotone. "Tritone" is similar to duotone, except three halftones are used.

The other option is to scan a black & white print as though it were color and create separation film as with a color original. The resulting color halftone separations can be used to make plates which can be printed in single halftone, duotone, tritone, or even four colors.

THE IMPORTANCE OF PAPER

No printing job will look better than the paper it is printed on. The cost of paper is a major component of the cost of any printing job, often as much as 30% or 40% of the job's total cost. There is a natural temptation to try to save money through buying less expensive paper. But with cards, posters and calendars, buying quality paper is extremely important. Do not skimp on it. Do not listen to printers who are not fully aware of the role quality paper stock plays in the salability of consumer paper products.

(From the printer's point of view, he makes no money on your paper purchase if you buy it directly, and only a slight mark-up if you buy it through him. He would rather see you spend money on printing.)

Generally, only the thicker and better sheets of paper will be suitable for card and poster reproduction. This means using "premium cover" paper stock. Two of the standard sizes for cover sheets are 20"X26" and 26"X40". Cover sheets are available with various "coatings" (finishes) including cast, dull and gloss. Art posters reproduce well on 80lb. dull coated cover stock. Cards print well on 12 point (or heavier) gloss cover stock. Premium enamel coated book stock in 70lb. text weight is an appropriate choice for a calendar.

Choice of the right paper for a given project is a complex matter involving design issues, aesthetics, production concerns and economics. Publishers must be educated on the topic. A number of books listed in the *Resources Section* contain helpful information about paper. The "Paper and Ink" chapter in *Getting it Printed* contains a particularly useful discussion. Generally, designers, printers and paper sales brokers are happy to help educate potential customers. They will have many sample books for you to look through. But paper and its terminology are potentially very confusing. To become really comfortable specifying paper for printing jobs takes actual experience. One possible way around this is to hire a knowledgeable and competent designer for your first couple of jobs. If you decide to do it yourself, read the books suggested in the *Resources Section*. Spend time researching paper. Ask many questions. Above all, trust your instincts. If a paper stock feels as if it will be too flimsy, it probably is not heavy enough.

SOME ALTERNATIVE PROCESSES

Most cards, posters and calendars sold commercially are published using the offset lithography process which has been described in this chapter. It is widely available, is capable of reproducing a tremendous range of artwork and is quite economically practical in quantities of 2,000 sheets or more.

However, there are other ways to produce paper products. Posters can be silk screened. Cards can be put together by hand in a number of ways.

What these alternative processes have in common is that they are essentially not used in mass production. On the positive side, this means that a card can be published without producing thousands of cards. No huge amount of money is needed to start publishing your artwork. Quite a few artists have been modestly successful at assembling products, particularly cards, by hand and distributing them in their locality.

The primary downside of a manual process is that it does require individual labor to make each unit. Mass distribution will probably never be possible because the true cost of the labor involved is too high. In the hands of a gifted artist, handmade items can be truly unique and wonderful. But without a gifted creator, the resulting product can appear to be simply sloppy and unprofessional.

Artists have been moderately successful with cards that are hand painted. Usually these are signed and numbered and sell for more than a normal greeting card.

Reproducing a photograph or other artwork as an inexpensive photographic print or photocopier print and then "tipping in" (applying adhesive to the corners) to a blank folding card has worked for some other artists. It is possible this way to create a hundred cards at a time rather than the thousands required by offset.

The emergence of the laser printer and suppliers such as PaperDirect, Inc. (see *Resources Section*) opens up a whole new world of short run production possibilities for the artist who understands computers, owns a laser printer, and is gifted with imagination. ◆

4.

Creating a Design for Publication

*T*hroughout *Publishing Your Art* various parts of the publishing job are discussed as though the task has been delegated to a distinct, professional individual as would happen in a large publishing company. For example, this chapter outlines the steps required to create a design for publication and assumes that a designer will be performing these steps. Often there will be no such person. A self-publishing artist will be forced to do many jobs for himself. This may include the job of designer. If so, the person wearing the hat of designer must fill the designer's shoes. The tasks that must be accomplished remain the same. In this book, different tasks will be referred to by their distinct titles, and described by function, although it is understood that one person may be wearing all the hats and filling all the jobs.

Free-lance designers are hired on a per-job basis. Fees should be negotiated in advance. The extent of an individual designer's involvement in a particular project varies widely. Sometimes a designer functions merely to flesh out ideas that have already been developed by the publisher. At other times, the designer is the true conceptualizer and creative force behind a product. Expectations regarding designer involvement (particularly supervision of production) should also be clarified before the designer is hired.

There is a great range in the fees charged by designers depending on their reputations, how busy they are, how long they think the job will take them, and how much they want to do a particular job. Good designers are skilled and creative individuals who do not belong to a union and do not have to work according to any particular pay scale. Charges for a particular job are very much the result of negotiation between publisher and designer. As in any business transaction, the best way for a purchaser to get an idea of what a job should cost is to get at least three arms-length estimates.

As of press date of this book, Wilderness Studio usually charges a design fee of between $500.00 and $1,000.00 for designing one fine art poster. Actual costs of approximately $200.00 are also passed on to the client. This includes the creation of a mechanical but not production supervision. Some designers might charge less than this and some more. We might decide to charge differently for a particular project. These figures are not intended to be the final word on design fees, but are provided to help the reader who is a novice with a starting place. The Graphic Artists Guild Handbook, *Pricing & Ethical Guidelines* (see *Resources Section*), is also worth looking at.

Designers should be selected based on their previous work, their portfolios, and their fees. Seeking the designer of products or pieces you admire is an excellent way to find someone good. Often publications, particularly books, carry design credits. In addition, many publishers will be happy to tell you who designed a particular project.

Do not expect to get advice from designers without paying for it. Beyond providing a very rough estimate, professional designers simply cannot afford to spend much time working on a project unless they know they have the job.

THE ROLE OF THE DESIGNER

The designer plays the following role in the production of cards, posters and calendars:

(1) Conceptualizes, articulates and sketches a design for the product based on the artwork, the specifications of the publisher, research into comparable successful products, and general principles of good design;

(2) Prepares accurate mock-ups of what the final printed job will look like for approval by the publisher. The complete simulation of a printed piece is known in the trade as a "comprehensive dummy," or "comp" for short;

(3) Plans all phases of the production of the product;

(4) Prepares the art for reproduction and a mechanical for the printer;

(5) Optionally, if the designer is hired to do so, he may oversee production (the actual printing job).

Sometimes a designer is hired to be an extension of the publisher and to create technically acceptable mechanicals based on the publisher's ideas. In this case the role of the designer is limited. He is functioning more as technician than as artist and may be called a "mechanical artist" rather than a designer.

However, in many other cases a designer will be hired because of past ability to deliver pieces with a distinctive look and a proven track record of designing work that is successful. A designer who has been hired to do a truly creative job must be given the freedom to do so. When you hire an established design professional, it is often for the "look" he creates. Within reason, expect him to do it his way. It makes no sense to fight your designer's look. If you do not like it, find another designer. Obviously, in the absence of schizophrenia, this potential conflict is nonexistent if the publisher is also the designer and artist.

GOOD DESIGN

Good design should be functional. Something that does not work is not functional and is not well designed. Something that falls apart before its time is also not well designed. The exterior design, or form of the object, should reflect its function. This means that an art poster should look like something intended to go on the wall. Greeting cards should take account of applicable postal regulations. They should look like they are intended to be mailed.

Amusing cards are probably well-designed if they appear amusing. Condolence cards are well designed if they convey sympathy. What is good design for one product with one function is not necessarily good design for another product with a different function.

Consistency of design can be very important to a company's line of products. Similar products should be designed uniformly in at least some respects. This means that a standard template for the information that will go on the piece should be developed. For example, the backs of most cards must have the trade name of the company in a standard typographic face ("font") as well as certain other information such as price coding and copyright notice. The advantage of this standardization is that it helps to increase brand recognition.

Be careful to allow sufficient space around an image. Designing white space in pleasing proportions is as important as sizing art well. Choose type fonts in a style and size that work well with imagery. The total width of the line(s) of type taken as a block should visually relate to the image size.

Do not mix many dif-

- Length of line of type relates to image width.
- Side/top border to bottom border proportion: ≈1:2½.

Poster text proportion illustrated.

ferent typefaces in one piece. With the arrival of desktop publishing it has become much easier and less expensive to do this than it used to be; it leads to crowded and unpleasant looking designs.

Usually, less is more. Good design does not call attention to itself. It stays in the background. It should never detract from the artwork it incorporates. Design that is noticed before the artwork is self-important

Printing Production Planner

(Check box when item is completed)

Function	Date	Supplier
☐ 1. Conceptualize Product		
☐ 2. Research Competition		
☐ 3. Research Distribution		
☐ 4. Conceptualize Artwork		
☐ 5. Create or Obtain Art		
☐ 6. Approve Visual Elements		
☐ 7. Write Text		
☐ 8. Edit Text		
☐ 9. Make Rough Layout		
☐ 10. Approve Rough Layout		
☐ 11. Make Formal Comps for Design Approval		
☐ 12. Specify Typography		
☐ 13. Set Type		
☐ 14. Create Mechanicals		
☐ 15. Approve Mechanicals		
☐ 16. Prepare Art for Reproduction		
☐ 17. Prepare Request for Quotation		

and not good. In addition, the effort that the design has taken should not be noticed. The best design seems simple and fluid and stays in the background. In the words of the poet Randall Jarrell, "Art, being bar-tender, is never drunk."

In some respects, life _is_ design. Everything can be thought of as design, and every-thing that exists has been designed (even

Function	Date	Supplier
❑ 18. Get Estimates from Printers		
❑ 19. Choose Printer and Separator		
❑ 20. Make Halftones/ Separations		
❑ 21. Approve Proofs of Separations		
❑ 22. Select Paper		
❑ 23. Approve Proofs from Printer		
❑ 24. Print Job		
❑ 25. Approve Press Sheets		
❑ 26. Bind and Finish Job		
❑ 27. Ship Job from Printer to Publisher		
❑ 28. Verify that Shipped Product is Acceptable		
❑ 29. Verify that Printer has Returned Art and Mechanicals		
❑ 30. Pay Printer and Other Trade Vendors		

Printing Production Planner
- page 2 -

if the cosmic design process is partially random). Design is a way of life. It cuts across disciplines. Much the same core creative abilities go into the design of gardens, houses, plumbing systems, computer programs, business cards, and books as go into the creation of cards, posters and calendars.

The best thing you can do is to educate yourself about design. Start a collection of well-designed things. Try to articulate what you like about the designs of these things. If something seems poorly designed, ask yourself, "Why? What would improve its design?" Pay particularly close attention to the design of products that are of the sort you would like to publish. What is good about the design of these products? What could be improved? Why was it done this way?

PLANNING

Detailed and careful planning of a print production job is extremely important to its successful conclusion. The checklist on pages 44 and 45 is presented to help organize card, poster and calendar printing jobs.

CREATING A MECHANICAL

A mechanical cannot be created until there is a clear picture of what the final published product is to look like. Before starting the mechanical, have the design completely sketched out, comped (the preparation of an accurate comprehensive dummy or mock-up), and approved.

The purpose of the mechanical is to provide a complete guide for the printer of how to prepare a particular job. In addition, the mechanical includes elements of a project that are not provided elsewhere in a form ready for reproduction (termed "camera-ready"). These elements are typically the typography and lines such as holding lines that will go around an image. Sometimes other forms of line-art are also included in the mechanical in camera-ready form.

Generally, a mechanical is presented with its elements pasted to a single board. Tissue overlays are often attached, both to protect the mechanical and to provide a place for written explanations.

A mechanical should include the following elements:

(1) Photostats or photocopier prints showing the precise placement and size of art;

(2) Camera-ready typography and other line-art, precisely positioned;

(3) Crop marks showing the final trim size of the finished piece; if the piece is to be scored or folded, that should also be indicated;

(4) Written instructions that include scaling information on the art and explain

anything that is not immediately obvious in the mechanical. It is a good idea to include the designer's name and phone number in case the printer has any questions. These instructions are placed on the tissue overlay or on a separate sheet of paper. In either case, it is extremely important that the instructions be well-attached physically to the mechanical board.

The two most important technical characteristics of a mechanical are absolute clarity (so that a printer can follow it with no possible misinterpretations) and crisp reproduction quality of camera-ready elements (particularly typography) that the

mechanical contains.

Before the desktop publishing revolution, which dates from the late 1980s, typography was ordered from catalogs of typefaces. Typographic companies then physically produced the type on complex and expensive machines dedicated to that purpose. Customers could specify the size of the type in "points" (there are seventy-two points to the inch). They could also specify a general setting for "kerning" (spacing between letters) and "leading" (spacing between lines). Often, these settings were not accurate enough. Different letters within a word needed to be kerned differently. The only way to achieve this was to physically

Illustration of a mechanical.

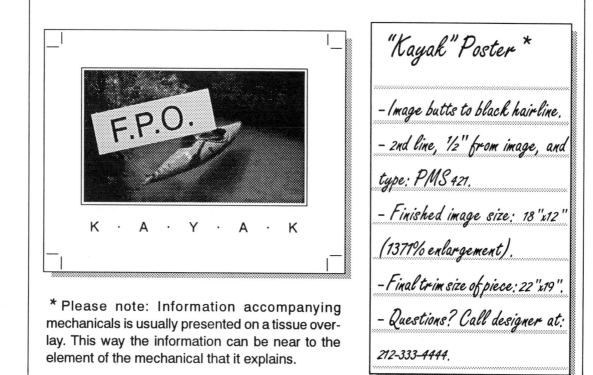

* Please note: Information accompanying mechanicals is usually presented on a tissue overlay. This way the information can be near to the element of the mechanical that it explains.

"Kayak" Poster *

- Image butts to black hairline.
- 2nd line, ½" from image, and type: PMS 421.
- Finished image size: 18"x12" (1377% enlargement).
- Final trim size of piece: 22"x19".
- Questions? Call designer at: 212-333-4444.

cut apart the typographic output and paste it by hand correctly spaced on the mechanical board.

Type can still be ordered in this fashion, and good typographers (these days called "Typographic Service Bureaus" or simply "Service Bureaus") will do their best to help fledgling designers. However, type and other elements of a design can be specified with far greater flexibility and accuracy on a desktop computer station. Once the design has been created, it is delivered to the service bureau as a computer file and run through a high resolution image setter. The image setter outputs camera-ready type. The "Using your Computer" section of this chapter contains further discussion of how to do this.

Service bureaus will also provide other services related to creating mechanicals. They are your best source for photostats. They will also adhere typographic and other elements to a board for you and provide the tissue overlay. You can also do this "paste-up" yourself. Hot wax or rubber cement is usually used to attach type to the mechanical board because they provide firm placement yet can be moved if necessary. But you may use any adhesive material you like if it works.

Don't use Elmer's; water-based glues tend to wrinkle output paper.

Service bureaus can be found in the Business Yellow Pages under "Typesetting." An excellent compact reference book that contains much of the technical information required to create mechanicals and includes a proportion wheel is *Graphics Master* (see *Resources Section*).

PREPARING ART FOR REPRODUCTION

To prepare art for reproduction, the designer must start with the actual artwork that will be used for film-making via a scanner or a process camera. (To keep this discussion simple, it will be assumed that color art is being prepared for separation on a scanner. All remarks apply equally to black and white art that will be screened using a process camera.) For example, if an oil painting is to be reproduced, the designer should be provided with the high quality photographic transparency of the painting that will actually be used for scanning. (There are commercial photography studios that specialize in photographing art for reproduction.) If a reproduction dupe (large format duplicate) made from a 35mm photographic original is to be scanned for separations, the designer should work from the actual reproduction dupe. If a photographic print is to be directly scanned, the designer will need the actual print to be used. The actual art that will be scanned <u>must</u> be used (for the sake of the balance of this discussion termed "original art"), or inaccuracies will invalidate the process.

The job of preparing art for reproduction involves three steps:

(1) The original art that is to be separated must be sized and scaled;

(2) The original art must be cropped;

(3) The sizing, scaling, and cropping should be double and triple checked. The original art must then be presented in the fashion that is conventional in the printing industry and contains no mistakes.

Assuming the designer is fairly well along in the process of creating a mechanical, he should know the dimensions that the art will have in the final piece. To scale artwork for reproduction means to find the percentage of enlargement or reduction, which, when applied to the original art, yields the dimensions desired in the mechanical. When you have found this number, you have "scaled" the art.

The first step is to obtain accurate measurements of the original <u>cropped</u> art and the final size. Next, convert any fractions of an inch to decimal notation, for example 10 1/16" to 10.0625". (If you are using the metric system, you won't have to make this conversion.) Taking one dimension, for example vertical, the following equations, where X is expressed as a percent-

An example of art prepared for reproduction.

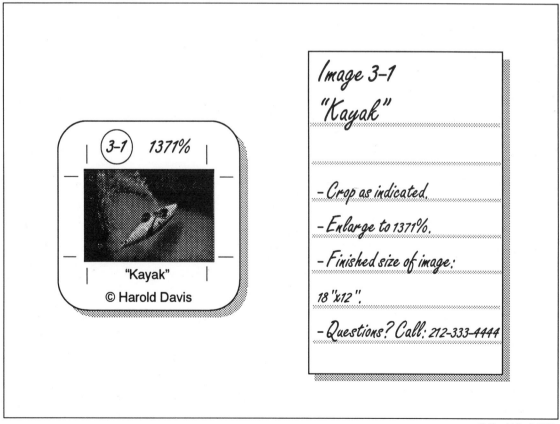

3-1 1371%

"Kayak"

© Harold Davis

Image 3-1
"Kayak"

- Crop as indicated.

- Enlarge to 1371%.

- Finished size of image:

18"x12".

- Questions? Call: 212-333-4444

age, will give you the proper scaling.

$$\frac{Final\ Size}{Original\ Size} = \frac{X}{100}$$

This can be rewritten as:

$$X = \frac{Final\ Size * 100}{Original\ Size}$$

However, it is sometimes helpful to keep it in the first form while making final adjustments to the scaling.

After the one dimension has been scaled (the vertical dimension for example), the other (horizontal) should also be scaled as a check on the accuracy of the first calculation.

Proportion wheels are used to calculate the same information. They can be found at any good art supply store (*Graphics Master*, mentioned above, includes one). The size of the original art is found on the inside, smaller wheel. This is then aligned to the finished size desired on the outside wheel. The percentage scaling ap-

pears in the window on the smaller wheel.

However, as one working designer notes, "Proportional wheels are all very well and good for initial estimates. However, for final mechanicals, I use a calculator. I don't want an irate printer calling me with the news that my scaling is off fractionally."

The same designer observes, "After a while you get a feeling for what proportional percentages should be in a given situation and will know if a scaling is off-the-wall." Calculating enlargements and reductions becomes much easier with experience.

Once the art has been scaled, a "stat" (an inexpensive black and white reproduc-

---

Illustration of a proportion wheel.

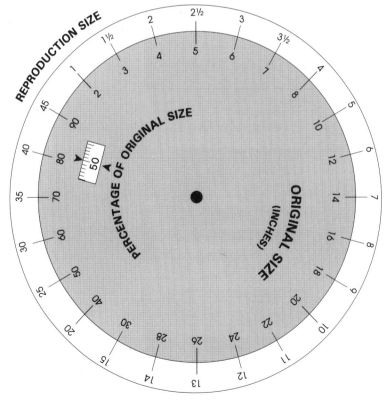

tion) should be ordered from your service bureau at the specified percentage enlargement. (A photocopier that enlarges can be used instead of a stat for reflected art.) The stat will be adhered to the mechanical in position to illustrate how the art is to be enlarged. It is very important to prominently mark the stat "fpo" or "for position only"; printers have been known to mistake material intended to show positioning for reproduction copy. The percentage of scaling should also be indicated. It is conventional to cut the edges of a stat or photocopier print to be used for positioning purposes in a wavy pattern before adhering it to the mechanical board. This helps ensure that the printer will know it is intended for positioning only.

The original art itself must be marked with cropping indications. If it is a transparency, place it in a clear plastic window, and tape the sides so that it cannot shift within the container. Use removable white drafting tape to lightly and carefully mark where it is to be cropped. Also use removable white drafting tape to mark cropping on prints, but be careful; if any of the tape sticks onto reproduction areas, it will appear in the final printed piece. Make sure to draw the crop lines well out in the margin of the prints.

Original art should be marked, on its sleeve or on its back, with percentage magnification and final reproduction dimensions. If the job involves a number of images, the art should be labeled with a letter or number that is keyed to the stat on the mechanical.

USING YOUR COMPUTER

Computers have made it a great deal easier to create mechanicals for reproduction. Almost without exception, they are heavily used by competent professional designers today. You can have, in your home, essentially the same tools used by top flight professionals. However, there are two warnings to novices:

(1) Desktop publishing ("DTP") software puts a tremendous range of techniques and design elements at your finger tips. It does not teach you to use these techniques and design elements wisely.

(2) Purchasing and maintaining a DTP system can be fairly expensive. There is an extensive learning curve. Unless you enjoy this sort of thing in and of itself, consider contracting out your design work to a professional who already has the hardware and software working.

Mechanicals can be effectively created on the Mac or PC-Windows platforms using page layout or illustration software. A good service bureau can produce output with equal ease from Mac and PC-Windows applications.

Large, text-based projects such as books are best done in a powerful page layout program such as PageMaker, Quark,

Ventura, FrameMaker, or MS-Publisher. Cards, posters and calendars are best done in applications such as Arts & Letters, CorelDraw and Illustrator, where the lack of effective multiple page handling is offset by powerful design tools.

The latest versions of powerful word processing programs such as Ami Pro, Word for Windows and WordPerfect for Windows have some design and page layout capabilities. However, do not attempt to create a mechanical using a word processing program. They will not produce satisfactory professional level designs because they lack adequate placement tools and cannot manipulate type with sufficient flexibility.

Newcomers to desktop publishing must keep it simple when it comes to using many typefaces in the same design. Before the DTP revolution, practical and economic limitations kept font use relatively restrained. Today, it is very easy to call up multiple fonts when using computers, but the results invariably look terrible. The fact that you can easily do so is no justification for actually doing it. Good design shows restraint. Nowhere is lack of education about good design more apparent than in DTP documents containing scores of different typefaces.

Currently, the fonts encoded in a format known as Type 1 PostScript have become the common standard in the typographic and typesetting service bureau industries. Files sent out for high resolution output should contain fonts only in this format.

Therefore, these are the only fonts you should use when creating mechanicals on your own computer. This means that to see a hard copy of what you are doing, you will need a Postscript, or Postscript compatible, laser printer attached to your computer. These laser printers output pages printed in low resolution (300-600 "dpi," or dots per inch). They are used to proof work as you go along. Once you are satisfied with the results, a computer file is sent via modem or transmitted on disk to the service bureau which outputs the material at high resolution (1200-2800 dpi).

Specific computer applications can best be mastered through practice and by reading manuals and handbooks. But, in very general terms, the following steps are required to create a mechanical on the computer:

(1) The application must be opened.

(2) A paper size and direction (portrait or landscape) must be selected. Using a proportion wheel or the formulas noted in the section on "Preparing Art for Reproduction," this size should be a workable proportion of the actual trim size of the finished design. It should print on your laser printer for proofing purposes.

(3) A rectangle should be created in scale place for imagery.

(4) Type should be placed in position to scale. Spacing, kerning and leading should be fine tuned.

(5) Crop marks should be added.

(6) The design should be printed at 300 dpi on your laser printer. Revise it if necessary.

(7) Once the low resolution version has been approved, re-scale all elements of the design. A note of caution: as elements are reproduced in higher resolution, they appear lighter as well as sharper. Hairlines and greyscale will be lighter or thinner. Lines that are visible at 300 dpi may be invisible at 2400 dpi. ½ point lines are the finest that will reliably show at high resolutions.

(8) Print the document to an Encapsulated PostScript (.eps) file on your hard drive. Generally, this is done in the Options Menu of the Print Command.

(9) Download the file via modem to a service bureau or copy it to a floppy disk and bring it to the service bureau.

Good service bureaus will help to educate you and guide you through any initial hurdles. Don't be afraid to ask questions. It is their job to tell you what you must know, and most of them take this educational function very seriously. The more their clients know about desktop publishing, the better customers they are.

THE DESKTOP PUBLISHING REVOLUTION AND ITS IMPLICATIONS

The Desktop Publishing revolution is only a few years old. In this short time, it has caused great changes in the printing, design and typography industries. The significance of these changes are just beginning to become apparent. Ultimately, they will rival the discovery of the printing press in importance and change many aspects of the way human beings deal with information.

In the context of publishing your art as cards, posters and calendars, the main impact at this point is to put vastly powerful design tools into everyone's hands. As little as a decade ago, these tools would have required great capital outlay to purchase and much technical education to use. Today, most people can afford to create their own designs. They have at their disposal a great battery of effects, tools and typefaces.

The danger is that there will be a flood of amateurish designs created with professional level tools. The hope is for an explosion of creativity and wonderful new designs powered by individuals as well as corporate giants. ◆

5.

Dealing with Printers and Other Graphic Arts Professionals

*R*eproducing art as cards, posters, and calendars—like most things in life—largely involves dealing effectively with people. The following are basic principles that apply to dealings with professional service vendors such as printers and others in the graphic arts.

■ Seek to create long-term relationships. Finding a supplier who works well with you year after year is far more important than getting an initial low price.

■ Behave with integrity yourself. You expect your printer to deliver as promised and make good for any possible mistakes. Keep your end of the bargain. Don't expect printers to do your job. For example, a printer should not be asked to make design decisions. Pay your bills as agreed.

■ Always get contracts, estimates and other important business arrangements in writing.

■ The only way to monitor the fairness of a printer's estimate is to get two alternate competitive estimates in writing, based on the identical written specifications supplied to the first printer.

■ Make sure that the printing organization you hire has the attitude, resources and experience to successfully finish your job.

CREATING PRINTING SPECIFICATIONS AND REQUESTING PRICE QUOTATIONS FROM PRINTERS

Printing specifications must be explained in writing. Specifications must be unambiguous so that estimates from different printers based on the specifications can be compared. Specifications should also be simple to understand and as clear as possible.

A specification is also known as a "Request for Quotation". The printer's response is termed either a "Quotation" or an estimate.

In order to accurately craft a printing specification, it is necessary to first fully understand the printing job. Usually, this means that specifications must be written after the art has been prepared and the mechanical has been created.

Printing specifications should include the following elements: quantity of finished pieces required; paper stock; trim size of the finished piece; the nature of the original art, scaling, and final size of the art; number of colors required; varnishes or coatings required; scoring, folding and special finishing instructions (if required); packing and shipping instructions; the contact name and phone number to call with questions.

The Request for Quotation reproduced on pages 56 and 57 was used by Wilderness Studio for an actual job. It can be used as a model for your own specifications.

While the estimates that you receive vary in formality, all include detailed pricing information based on your specifications. A printer's estimate is called a "Quotation". (See sample Quotations that respond to the Request for Quotations, pages 56-60.) Designer Liane Sebastian recommends creating your own form. She says, "If they choose, they can still send me their forms with mine, but I make sure each fills out mine so that I don't have to spend time I don't have trying to put them in the same context."

Some elements of the pricing in a Quotation may depend on choices you have yet to make. (In the example above, the printer is asked to quote in a quantity of 2,500 and also additional thousands. The price is also to be given with and without separations.) The quotation should provide all numbers requested and point out the variable contingencies. But it will not always happen; the sample quotation (pages 58 and 59), in response to the sample specification, ignores the requested units and quotes on the basis of 2,500 and 5,000. The less formal Quotation (page 60) also ignores the 5,000 requested unit quote and simply gives an $0.85 per unit additional cost after the first 2,500.

If the quotation contains the information you need, this level of imprecision is not significant. If it doesn't contain that information, request a revision.

Generally, quotations are valid for thirty or sixty days. Technically, this will depend on the boilerplate language on the back of the printer's quotation form and applicable commercial legal practice. If a quotation has not been accepted during this period, it lapses and can no longer automatically be assumed to be valid.

As a practical matter, printers need business. They will honor a quotation for a reasonable amount of time, but not forever.

As the sample Printer's Estimate suggests,

the forms and contents of Quotations will vary. Careful analysis, facilitated by using a standard "Request for Quotation" (below), is required. It is important that projects be planned sufficiently in advance so that there is enough time to fully understand estimates. Any terms that you do not understand on the "Quotation"

Sample Request for Quotation

Wilderness Studio

Street Adress
City, State 00000

Date

REQUEST FOR QUOTATION

To: Paul Printer
Paul Printing Company
via fax 111-222-3333, pages=2

Dear Sir or Madam:

Please provide a written quotation on the printing or finishing service(s) as specified below. Any questions may be addressed to Harold Davis at the above address and telephone. Note that Wilderness Studio is primarily a publisher of art reproductions and posters; all work is therefore expected to be of premium or showcase quality.

PROJECT TITLE: "Denali the Great One, Alaska", Reprint
OUR STOCK #: WS102
QUANTITY REQUESTED: 2.5M + additional thousands
ART PROVIDED: Please quote two ways: (1) Camera Ready Mechanical + loose separation film of 4/c image ready for imposition; (2) Camera Ready Mechanical + 4"X5" transparency for 4/c (image area 19"X30") (e.g., sep to be provided by printer)
Mechanical: see above

Line Art Provided: n/a

FORMAT: Trim Size: Approx. 25"X35" (see sample)
HALFTONES (if required): n/a
DUOTONES: n/a

should be fully explained by the printer. If there are any inconsistencies or omissions, you should request a revision of the quotation. A less formal Printer's Estimate, based on the same specifications, appears below.

Sometimes there is a great disparity be-

Request for Quotation
- page 2 -

SEPARATIONS (if required):

☑ From transparency   ☐ From reflected copy

Note: <u>Quote should be based on both doing the sep and without doing the sep (see above)</u>
Size Original; Finished size of sep; % Magnification:4"X5" to 19"X30" approx. 500% scaling

Proofs Required: Chromalin or equivalent

STOCK: 80lb. dull coat cover premium stock - please provide sample.

Paper: Weight: Finish:

☑ Send Paper Sample   ☐ Buy Paper From:

PRINTING:
# of sides: 1
# of colors: 4 + 2 touch plate PMS (if necessary)
Varnish(es):   Image spot gloss varnish + border matte varnish
PMS or other special: See above

SPECIALTY PRINTING: n/a
BINDING: n/a

PACKING & SHIPPING: Pack posters in groups of 100 in sturdy cartons or well-wrapped thick cardboard wrapped packages; load on pallet(s); ship to our warehouse, Glen Head, NY 11545; indicate shipping costs in estimate.

COMMENTS: See sample provided on request.

---

tween price quotes by different printers in their estimates on the same project. In this case, if the printers, in your judgment, are roughly of the same caliber, the difference should be called to the attention of the printer with the higher prices. He should be asked to explain. Perhaps when confronted with a

Sample Printer's Estimate

Paul Printing Company
100 Main Street
Any City, No State 11111

QUOTATION

Date

Harold Davis
Wilderness Studio
New York, NY

Dear Harold:

It is our pleasure to provide the following preliminary estimate for the project described in your Request for Quotation.

DESCRIPTION: "Denali, the Great One," fine art poster reprint
CLIENT PREPARATION: (1) Camera-ready mechanical and loose separation film of 4/C image ready for imposition; OR (2) Camera ready mechanical and 4"X5" transparency for 4/C (image area 19"X30"). In case (2), Paul Printing Company will do the separation.

TRIM SIZE: 34½ "X 24 13/16"
COLORS: 4/Color process + PMS black and gloss & matte varnish off line
STOCK: 80# LOE Dull Coat Cover
BINDING: Trim to size and pack into sturdy cartons of 100 per carton
PROOFS: Composed match prints
SHIPPING: F.O.B. Paul Printing Company, Any City, No State
QUANTITY: 2,500 - 5,000

© Harold Davis 1993.

lower, competitive estimate, he will adjust prices downward. However, the other possibility is that the lower priced printers are trying to take shortcuts that may damage the ultimate quality of the job.

When you decide to hire a printer for a

Quotation
Harold Davis
- Page 2 -

PRICE:

	(1) 4/C supplied	(2) Paul Printing to supply 4/C
	2,500 - $4,650.00	2,500 - $5,510.00
	5,000 - $6,400.00	5,000 - $7,260.00

Shipping costs to Glen Head, NY

2,500	5,000
$150	$210

Prices are based on current paper costs. Final pricing will be based on the prevailing cost of paper when it leaves the mill.

Thank you for giving us the opportunity of submitting an estimate for this project. We look forward to the possibility of working with you. Please feel free to contact me if you have any questions.

Sincerely,

Paul Printer

Paul Printer
Vice President, Sales

Enclosure: Paper Sample

project, the printer should be informed both in writing and verbally. Generally, written notification is done with a "Purchase Order" which may simply include the quantity needed and reference the "Quotation" (see pages 58-59 and below). Of course, if large sums of money are involved, your paperwork should be checked by a knowledgeable attorney.

(see pages 58-59 and below)

SPECIALTY CARD AND POST CARD SHOPS

Some printers are set up to exclusively print one kind of item. By concentrating on their specialty, configuring their plant for it, and purchasing paper for their specialty in vast bulk, they can produce their

Sample Printer's Estimate, Brief Version

Less Formal Printing Company
Any Street
Any City, Any State

To: Harold Davis
        Wilderness Studio
        Your Denali Poster Production

$650	Separation
$400	Stripping (Creating special Burns)
$6006	Plates
$2,900	2,500 delivered prints, packed in hundreds Additional salable prints 0.85¢ each.
$2,069	Paper cost (4,000 sheets of 10pt dull coated $517/M)
$6,619	Total

Call if questions—

Leon Less Formal

© Harold Davis 1993.

sole product very economically. A good example of this is the many printing companies who produce #10 business envelopes, with and without windows, imprinted with the return address in one font-style in black.

Similarly, there are quite a few specialty printing shops that produce brochures, greeting cards, and post cards. Generally, from the best of these shops you can expect only acceptable quality printing, nothing better. Your choice of paper stock, final trim size, ink, and finishes will be limited by the printer's stock on hand and formatting guidelines. However, if you supply your own mechanical (as opposed to having the

Sample Simple Purchase Order

Wilderness Studio
Street Address
City, State 00000

PURCHASE ORDER

To: Paul Printing Company
100 Main Street
Any City, No State 11111

2,500 "Denali, the Great One" Posters per your Quotation of (date)

BY:

_____
Authorized Signature

specialty shop do it) the design of the finished piece can be customized to your taste.

Usually, the unit cost of cards produced by specialty shops will be too high to profitably distribute and resell the cards. A lower unit cost is achieved by increasing the size of print runs and by producing your own flats consisting of many cards which are cut apart after printing. Printing shops that specialize in standardized cards are catering to consumers who have need for a few thousand of a <u>single</u> card. They should not be considered as suppliers of a salable product for a publisher. They are often located in remote parts of the country and generally deal with their customers by UPS and telephone.

Examples of the appropriate customers for specialty card printers are artists who need an exhibition announcement card and artists who want to do a mailing of a single card to art directors to promote their work.

If you decide to have a specialty shop print a card of yours, be sure to allow plenty of time. These operations are slow, may print specific items only at specific times, and charge a premium for faster delivery. Contact the printer well in advance for his schedule and kit describing pricing and formats available. Design your card to fit into the closest available format that the printer offers. While most of these specialty printers will prepare your mechanical at a nominal cost, do it yourself or

have someone local do it instead. It is generally a mistake to entrust your design work to an assembly-line printer.

GETTING GOOD COLOR SEPARATIONS

Your printer can handle your color separations for you, or you can deal directly with a separator. Some printers have in-house separation facilities; others subcontract the work to outside vendors.

The most important thing you can do to insure a good quality separation is to supply the separator with high quality original artwork. At a minimum, artwork should be clean and sharp. For further information on the preparation of art for separating, see "Separations and Spot Color" in Chapter 3 and "Preparing Art for Reproduction" in Chapter 4.

Today, printing and separating are aspects of the reproduction process with a very different *feel.* Suppliers of each tend to reflect that different feel. Printing is messy; separating requires antiseptic cleanliness. Hands-on blue collar laborers in ink and oil stained overalls fiddle with noisy and smelly printing presses. White-coated technicians sit at computer consoles and manipulate the laser scanners and computers that control the separation process.

The first time you work with a particular

separator you will know nothing about the separator's ability to deliver quality work other than what you have heard by word of mouth and what you have seen in the samples that the separator's salespeople have shown you. Of course, since the samples are being displayed to close a sale, they should be superb. Walk away immediately without doing business with any separator whose salespeople show you work for which they have to apologize. (Incredibly, this does happen. "They were a little off-register on the printing press," is a typical excuse.)

Generally, samples will be presented to you either as proofs of separations or in final printed pieces. Viewing actual proofs is a little purer because the quality of the printing job does not come into play, but many separators prefer to show completed prestigious printing projects. In either case, judging the quality is a matter of using your eyes and your common sense. Look out for dust or other flaws (called "hickies"). Make sure registration problems do not affect the sharpness of the image. A loop or magnifying glass may help with this. Check to see that the colors in the image appear crisp and pleasing.

After you have handed the artwork over to be separated, your next chance for participation in the process will be when you are asked to approve "loose proofs" made from the separation films. They are termed "loose proofs" because they have not yet been assembled with type and other design elements. Loose proofs gen-

erally appear on a plastic highly reflective material and go by various trade names including "Matchprints" and "Chromalins."

When viewing proofs, remember that color is a matter of taste. The important thing is for you to like the results. To ensure that, review proofs under balanced light conditions. If you compare the proof to the original art, make sure both are viewed under light of the same color temperature.

Some minor corrections to first proofs are normal; do not hesitate to require them. If you do not know technical color terminology, don't worry. Use English. Tell the separator, "The skin tones are too green," or whatever. Look for small problems in the separations such as hairs, dirt and dots. While these may just be on the surface of the proof, alert the separator and the printer to the possible problem.

Never, never accept a separation proof that you are displeased with. Often, a separator will claim that the thing you are unhappy about will be fixed on press. While a great deal of first aid is possible on press when it is in the hands of a skilled press operator, your life will be much easier (and less expensive) if you have a separation and proof that do not need correction on press. A good separator probably can accomplish anything reasonable using state of the art digital technology as long as he is told firmly, clearly, and specifically what to do.

GOING "ON PRESS"

The penultimate step of the reproduction process, and the most thrilling of the whole ride, is termed going "On Press." The publisher goes to the printer's premises and approves a printed sheet or sheets containing cards, posters or calendars following the make-ready. After the sheet has been approved, termed the "Press Okay," the thousands of sheets that make up the actual press run are printed to (at least in theory) exactly match it.

Although it is to the benefit of both printer and publisher to have the publisher present during the press phase, when this is not practical, the press okay is handled by an official of the printing company, usually the Production Manager. Large publishing companies have employees—generally assistants in the design or production departments—whose job is to approve press runs at the printer. Going on press can take a great deal of time. Not only is there physically getting to the printing plant, but press schedules are complex and can change at the last minute. Printing presses break down, need to be adjusted, and need to be cleaned in the middle of jobs. If you go on press and it takes a long time, the printing company will try to keep you as happy as possible. But they are used to press okays being performed by subordinate employees of the publisher whose job is to wait without complaint. Expect the process to take time.

If the publisher, or his representative, is present during the on press phase, he can personally make aesthetic judgments during the make-ready process. He can also correct errors before it is too late. The benefit to the printer is that once there has been a press okay, provided the printed sheets match the one that has been approved, there can be no argument about the acceptability of the job.

The physical environments in which clients are expected to approve press runs vary tremendously. Sometimes it occurs as the press is running in an atmosphere of noise and fumes. At other shops, a comfortable room is set apart for clients who are approving jobs. In these shops, the client is encouraged to avoid the printing press area itself. Printed sheets are brought up during the make-ready process for comments and approval.

As with every other stage of viewing art in the reproduction process, care should be taken to view press sheets only under properly balanced light. Printers will be equipped to provide you with appropriate viewing conditions. Examine sheets carefully for small flaws such as dust and hickies and lack of sharpness. Circle any flaws you find on the sheet.

Color balance itself is a subjective matter. The printed piece should always be able to match the color as it appears in the separation proof. If you are aiming for something not exactly like the proof, you must be aware that there are limitations in what can be done with an offset press. Changing one color might affect the way something else looks. You must respect the expert opinions of the professionals around you about what can be done and what the options are. Do not demand the impossible. Be calm but decisive. Press time is too valuable to waste.

If all goes well with the make-ready and you are able to approve a press sheet, what a thrill! Your art is being reproduced—beautifully!

Once there has been a press okay and the rest of the sheets are printed, the job is packed and finished and sent to the publisher. A complete checklist of all steps in the print reproduction process from start to finish will be found on pages 44 and 45.

After reproduction has been completed, and the finished pieces have been shipped to the publisher, the next step is for the publisher to sell and distribute the printed pieces. The remainder of this book will examine this distribution process. From the point of view of the artist, how is work sold to existing publishers? Or, is the artist better off self-publishing? How do publishers arrange sales and distribution? How does art that is published as cards, posters and calendars get out into the world? ◆

6.

How to Find Greeting Card Publishers for your Work

Visual artists should follow industry protocol and exhibit courtesy and common sense every time they submit their work. This chapter provides general information about how to make a successful submission. Information about the greeting card industry that the artist who wishes to get work published must know is also included. (The material on the card industry will also be of interest to self-publishers; they should read it before jumping to Chapter 7, which is devoted to the topic of self-publishing cards.)

MORE ABOUT THE GREETING CARD INDUSTRY

Important properties of greeting cards as products are tremendous variety, topical sensitivity, low per unit profitability and great moneymaking potential for outstanding cards with good distribution.

Some greeting cards are timeless and never change. (A good example of this is the Hallmark "pansy card" reproduced on page 83, which was first published in 1939 and has continued to be one of Hallmark's best sellers ever since.) Other greeting cards are created in response to the latest social trends and jokes and go off the market after an evanescent and (possibly) spectacular life.

Greeting card companies range in size from the solo artist who sells handmade cards himself to museum and quality craft stores to huge corporate entities who sell millions of cards to supermarkets and mall shops.

Probably the greatest determinant of the commercial success or failure of a greeting card product line is the effectiveness (or lack of it) of the existing distribution network available to the publisher. Distribution arrangements in the greeting card industry vary as widely as everything else; this and the next chapter will examine these arrangements in considerable detail. The single most important thing to have in place if you are considering publishing your art as cards is a distribution network. Understanding card distribution is also crucial to getting your work published. If you are negotiating a licensing arrangement with an existing card publisher who wants to use your art, to effectively do so you must understand the fundamentals of distribution in the greeting card industry, the particular card company's distribution network, and the company's distribution plans for your product.

Perhaps the most formative feature of the greeting card industry is the low, in absolute dollars and cents terms, profit per unit. This is particularly true for small publishers. A per unit net profit of a nickel is doing well. Publishing companies must sell many cards to make any real money, and the fee or royalty they can afford to pay for art must necessarily be limited. Of course, many cards do sell very well (a card that sells 10,000 or more copies is considered a hit), and quite a few card companies are extremely profitable. But it takes publishing in volume, having an extremely good product, and having excellent distribution to become successful.

Fledgling card publishers will soon discover a certain Catch-22 regarding distribution: to make money, good distribution is required. To obtain good distribution, a network of excellent territorial sales "reps" is required. To get and keep

quality "reps", product with a track record is required. This barrier to entry-level publishing, and possible ways around it, will be discussed in detail in the next chapter, "Self-Publishing and Distributing Cards." Readers should file it in their minds as an important operating force in the card industry. One consequence is that large companies, with in-house distribution (e.g. sales "reps" who work solely for the one company) and "captive rack space" arrangements, can often nudge out smaller businesses.

Another important factor involves economy of production scale. With an essentially pre-sold captive rack space market, larger press runs are financially justified. Larger press runs lower unit costs. It is thus simply cheaper for the large companies to manufacture their product. Since unit costs are less, profit is higher. One consequence is that the large companies have more money to put into the constant new product development demanded by consumers of the greeting card industry.

Truly high volume card sales are probably not possible without captive rack space distribution arrangements.

Fundamentally, there is only one thing small publishers have working for them. Companies that can afford large press runs, in-house distribution staff, and captive rack space arrangements are generally part of late Twentieth Century monolithic corporate culture. They are usually not good at moving quickly, responding with sensitivity to social issues of the day or investing in eccentric visual ideas. Successful cards that are unusual, offbeat or timely are usually the product of small companies.

The personal image-defining function of cards, as well as public delight in some quirky, eccentric and well-designed products, create a window of opportunity for small niche publishers and their artists. (Of course, these publishers can expect to be copied by the big companies once they are successful enough.)

Artists should keep in mind (as publishers do) that for cards to sell they must first fit in racks in stores. This means that vertical designs have slightly more desirability than horizontal images for use as cards, simply because the vertical cards will take up less of the valuable rack space. It is extremely important to keep rack display issues in mind when presenting work to publishers—and when publishing.

HOW TO GET WORK PUBLISHED AS CARDS

Second only to creating truly publishable art, the most important steps you can take to get your work published involve effective research and planning. Research and planning for licensing is different from research and planning for self-publishing, which will be discussed in the next chapter.

Effective research for licensing imagery should answer these questions: What companies are the best publishers of my work? How do they fit into the card industry? What is their distribution? Try to target publishers whose current product line includes material that is in basic harmony with yours but is not exactly the same as yours. (The reason for this should be obvious. If they publish nothing even remotely close to yours, they probably won't want yours. If they already have something identical to yours, they won't need yours.)

Effective planning involves answering these questions: How should the publishers identified as targets best be approached? What are these publishers' needs? How would publication with them fit in with the artist's overall career plans?

There are two different kinds of arrangements that can be made with publishers. The most common involves simply licensing art on a one card, or card by card, basis. In the greeting card industry, this arrangement will generally not involve royalties. (Financial aspects of licensing are further discussed in the final section of this chapter.)

It is also possible to make an arrangement with a publisher under which you deliver an entire product line. This can be done only if you have successfully identified a genuine market need for a particular product line that you are in a better position than the publisher is in to provide. (One example of being in a better position than the publisher is in to provide a product line would be if you are the only artist in the world capable of making it.) A complete product line generally has a conceptual as well as a visual basis. It may contain work of more than one artist. An artist putting together a product line is functioning as a sort of consultant or packager, using his knowledge and contacts on behalf of the publisher. Generally, you should be well compensated for putting together a product line for a publisher; this compensation should include some form of royalty on sales.

Research on cards is best done by becoming a card hound. Visit card stores. Spend your life in card stores! Learn to recognize publishers and artists. Check price coding on the back of cards. Collect cards you like. Talk to card store owners and salespeople.

The National Stationery Show is the leading greeting card industry trade convention. It takes place at the Javits Convention Center in New York City in the late spring every year. An intensive visit is a very good way to learn about the greeting card industry fast. (While this show is "trade only", it should be fairly easy to generate appropriate business credentials. A professional artist's business card will probably suffice.)

Greetings Magazine is a publication with low production values and trade information about the industry. It will keep you abreast of many trends and new product releases.

Annual directories such as the *Artist's Market* and *Photographer's Market* published by Writer's Digest Books contain sections of listings of card publishers looking for art.

Hopefully, your research will identify some target publishers for your work. How should they be approached? Follow the protocol suggested in the next section, "Making a Submission." Select the actual imagery you include in the submission based on what your research has revealed about a particular publisher's needs. (Always be sure to also include some of your best work if it is different from work selected on the basis of an assessment of the publisher.)

Keep an accurate log of your submissions, and do not get discouraged by rejection. Often, rejection of your work is in fact not personal although it can certainly feel that way. It may have more to do with business factors entirely beyond your knowledge and control than the merit of your work. Try to use each rejection as a learning experience, and be prepared to send your submission back out again to another publisher as soon as it is returned.

If you are submitting a proposal for a product line as opposed to individual imagery, it may be appropriate to deviate from the standard submission protocol. You may want to write a formal marketing proposal, create mock-ups of the actual product, and approach industry contacts directly. Generally, a successful submission of this sort requires a prior track record and detailed knowledge of the industry.

No artist should expect to make a living solely by licensing imagery to the greeting card industry. (Any artist good enough to do so will surely be presented with other opportunities along the way.) This implies that it is essential to plan how greeting card sales will fit in with the rest of your career.

MAKING A SUBMISSION

It makes good sense to follow proper protocol when submitting work to publishers.

Take care to always be polite to everybody at the company to which you are submitting work. Even receptionists can be surprisingly important.

A certain amount of polite persistence is acceptable, but don't push too hard. Contrary to myth and Hollywood movie, excessive pushiness is usually counter-productive. A good product (read: artist) sells itself. No means no. Your work might simply be inappropriate for a given project. The art director might intend to keep you in mind for another product line at a future date. If you are sufficiently obnoxious, he may be more inclined to forget you in disgust.

Material submitted to publishers should always be duplicates. There is never a valid reason for submitting irreplaceable originals. Unsolicited submissions should always be accompanied by a self-addressed, stamped envelope ("S.A.S.E.") of adequate size for the return of your work.

The first step is to contact the publisher by telephone and find out the preferred submission format. Some companies will be very flexible. A few will even set up appointments to review your portfolio with you present. But most publishers will not want you there, and many will prefer to see duplicate slides. If in doubt, keep it simple. If you have no other guidelines from the company itself, send a sheet of twenty duplicate slides. Every slide should be labeled neatly with your name. (It is amazing how many people neglect this step thereby making clear their amateur status.)

It is good discipline to keep initial submissions to twenty images. This number is enough to present a quantity of different images and to show what you are capable of doing without satiating the publisher. If your initial presentation teases the publisher into requesting your full portfolio, then you have succeeded. (And think how embarrassing it could be to submit all your good work and then have nothing good left when they want to see the rest!) Remember that less is often more. "If you are really good, and know how good you are, six pictures should be enough," states Paul Gottlieb, Publisher of Harry N. Abrams, Inc.

A brief biography and explanatory statement about your work may be included. A reprint or two of an art magazine article would be best. Do not include a long, multi-paged resume. A short one-paged narrative summary that notes related publication credits is acceptable.

A cover letter should accompany the submission. Keep a copy. It should include your name, phone number, address and a brief description and quantity of slides submitted. Also note any related publication credits in the cover letter.

Give some care to packaging the submission. Packaging need not be elaborate, but should be thoughtful. It is a reflection of you and an extension of your work; the submission is being sent to a publisher operating in a visual and design conscious industry. There is at least a chance that the appearance and condition of your packaging will be noted.

FINANCIAL AND LEGAL CONSIDERATIONS

There are two kinds of licensing arrangements to consider. One involves the creation of an entire product line (see discussion of this in the section of this chapter on "How to Get Work Published"). If you enter into an agreement to create an entire product arrangement, your contract should be reviewed with care by an attorney, accountant or professional business advisor (possibly all three, if appropriate).

The other, more common, arrangement will be discussed here. It is the licensing of artwork on an image by image basis.

Unless there is a contrary contractual agreement, the creator of a work of art is the owner not only of the work but also of its copyright. The copyright to a work of art can be thought of as including a whole bunch of different rights that the owner can dispose of as he sees fit. For example, the following are both possible licenses to use a single work of art: "Exclusive worldwide reproduction rights in all media," and, "One-time reproduction rights as a greeting card in a press run of fewer than 10,000 copies." Obviously, there are problems when licenses granted to use a single image overlap or are contradictory, as in the example above.

Most often, publishers in the greeting card industry acquire licenses for, "exclusive greeting card reproduction rights," which should be limited in duration, for example, "Exclusive greeting card reproduction rights for three years." Artists should read the language of the license carefully. Do not give away too much. Do not give away something you do not have to give. Do not accept something you do not understand. Make all arrangements in writing. Limit press run size so that if the card is an unexpected hit you will share some of the proceeds. It usually makes good sense to get expert advice before a final agreement is signed.

As a practical matter, the language of the license is often handled rather informally.

It may appear on the publisher's purchase order to the artist or on the artist's invoice to the publisher. Another possible place for the language to appear is in a publisher's letter to the artist.

Compensation for artwork to be used as a greeting card can be as a flat fee or as a non-refundable advance against royalties. Amounts vary widely depending on the publisher, anticipated extent of distribution, and the fame of the artist. Royalty arrangements are comparatively rare in the greeting card industry partially because

Sample Simple Licensing Agreement
(for card use on an artist's invoice)

Joan Artist
100 Main Street
Anywhere, USA

INVOICE

DATE

To: Humongous Card Company
Street Address
City, State & Zip

License to reproduce my painting title "Gawking"
as a greeting card $500.00

Terms of license: Per your letter dated 1/3/94, by payment of this Invoice you will receive exclusive greeting card reproduction rights to this image in the United States, for a period of three years from the date of this Invoice, provided that the cumulative total of the press runs for the card does not exceed 10,000 copies.

Also note: 100 free artist's copies to be shipped to Joan Artist's studio at your expense; the 4"X5" reproduction chrome I have provided will be returned in good condition following separation.

© Harold Davis 1993.

---

of the expense involved in tracking the sales of a low-priced item. One card publisher states, "I pay a flat fee for the use of art. It is simply not the norm to pay royalties in this industry. Since I can get work from most other artists without paying royalties, generally I would not even consider working with one who demanded them."

In any case, royalty arrangements in the greeting card industry pose grave verification problems for artists. Most card companies would be unwilling to open their books to artists, and there are no standardized methods of keeping track of card sales. Unlike the book publishing industry—which has royalty verification problems of its own—bar code accounting for card sales is only partially implemented.

Where royalties are involved, the non-refundable advance should be equivalent to at least one year's worth of anticipated royalties.

Royalties can be expressed as a percentage of either the retail or the wholesale price of the card. They are equivalent if the retail percentage is half the wholesale percentage since the retail price is twice the wholesale price. But never enter into an arrangement that gives royalties on <u>net</u> profits. The calculation of net profits is entirely subject to the manipulation of the publisher. (A notorious public demonstration of this involves the block buster movie hit *Coming to America*. During the course of litigation, its studio, the movie

industry analog to publisher, reported a negative net profit on gross sales of over one hundred twenty million dollars. No amount of gross sales will ever insure a net profit when you do not control the accounting.)

The cleanest—because it is the least susceptible to manipulation—way to do it is to calculate royalties based on retail price, although these percentages will seem lower than wholesale royalty rates. The range of royalties in the card industry, when they are offered at all, is from 1% of retail to 4% of retail (equivalent to 2% of wholesale to 8% of wholesale).

The Graphic Artists Guild 1991 *Pricing & Ethical Guidelines* (see *Resources Section*) suggests a flat fee range for a greeting card design of between $400-$600. The American Society of Media Photographers (ASMP) 1983 survey of stock photography prices quotes a $250-$425 price range for a two-year greeting card license limited to the United States. World rights are an additional 50%. While the ASMP pricing survey is dated, stock pricing has not risen greatly in the last decade. In fact, these figures are probably toward the upper end of the scale for greeting card usage. A realistic range of flat fees that can be obtained in the greeting card industry is from $50.00 to $750.00. The upper end of this range is rare and will be achieved only by artists with a reputation of working with large publishers. How much you get will depend on your negotiating skills, how much the publisher wants to use your work, and the publisher's financial resources. The only thing you can be sure of is that a publisher's initial offer is probably not the best you can do. It is not uncommon for a greeting card company to start with an offer of $50-$75 per image (often many images are involved) but, in fact, be prepared to go to the $200 to $300 range if necessary. This last range is probably close to the average per-image greeting card flat fee license. Generally, publishers will, in addition, give the artist a substantial number of copies (up to 100) of the cards they publish for the artist's own use.

For the artist, licensing artwork for use as cards is an excellent way to earn income and exposure with very little effort and no investment. Working with greeting card publishers is a great way to gain professional experience and credentials while building up your portfolio and making money. If you do decide to go on and self-publish your art as cards, working first with a publisher on a licensing basis is a great way to learn about the industry. ◆

7.

Self-Publishing and Distributing Cards

*T*his chapter will examine business issues that the self-publisher of cards must tackle and overcome to succeed. Problems specific to the start-up card industry publisher—distribution and creating a "repping" organization—will be discussed in depth. More about the business of self-publishing will be found in Chapter 11, *A More Detailed Look at the Self-Publishing Option.* Chapter 11 provides information that applies to almost anyone thinking of starting any business. In contrast, this chapter focuses on the economics of starting a self-publishing card business. The crucial role of the independent sales representative is also discussed in detail.

The chapter concludes with an interview and profile of Jeff Milstein, whose Paper House Productions is a successful card publishing business. As Milstein puts it, "All other things being equal, I prefer to publish cards that use my photographs as opposed to the work of another. After all, taking the photographs is the fun part!"

THE ECONOMICS OF SELF-PUBLICATION OF CARDS

The purchase and transmittal of a card is a statement by the consumer both in terms of the specific message conveyed in the card ("Be mine tonight . . . ") and, more generally, about the taste of the purchaser. Art that is successfully used in cards recognizes this personal image-defining function of the media. Cards are purchased, consciously or unconsciously, based on the question, "What will the recipient think this says about me?" This primary purchasing motivation means that the card is a consumer product whose success or failure will almost completely depend on design and style. What is highly unusual about greeting cards as design-based products are their low retail unit prices. Most products in which design and style play a large role are usually luxury, expensive items.

We have already noted that low retail price

and profit per unit are perhaps the most formative features of the greeting card industry. Low unit profitability is particularly true for small publishers. The arithmetic of per-unit profit will be discussed in detail later in this section. For now, consider a card which retails for a fairly typical $1.50. (Incidentally, almost all cards are price-coded on their backs. Browsing in card stores and in card racks should give you a feel for retail price ranges. Note the differences in production values or the sizes of the card that can lead to a greater or lesser retail price.) The small publishing company will have done well to make a net profit of $0.05 on the $1.50, not including fees or royalties for the use of art. A company must sell a great many cards with only a nickel profit each to make any real money. Of course, many cards <u>do</u> sell very well (a card that sells 10,000 or more copies is considered a hit), and quite a few card companies are extremely profitable. But it takes publishing an extremely good product and having excellent distribution to be successful and is not something to be counted on.

While starting a card publication business has much in common with starting any kind of business, in some important ways the economics of card publication is distinctive.

The business of publishing cards involves <u>publishing</u>. It is typical to expect a publishing business to require an initial outlay of capital up front with return of the investment over a long period. Generally, a publishing business will not really prosper without a thriving "back list." ("Back list" in the book publishing industry means books that are not current releases but are in print.) It takes time to develop a successful back list. Managing a back list requires attention to inventory and a mechanism for handling many different product items. It also requires long-term intelligent creativity to assess objectively which products have the staying power to continue selling over time. Like other kinds of publishing businesses, card publishing requires acumen on the part of the publisher in creating and putting together product that has back list potential as well as planning an economic strategy.

The successful self-publisher of cards must find a way to create a product line that is unique in the marketplace. A product that is similar to a line that is already in the stores cannot succeed. (When Hallmark or another big company brings out a product that imitates the work of a small publisher it is different because of the substantial marketing muscle behind the derivative product.) A new self-publishing venture requires a niche of its own. Finding a niche of this sort is not an easy thing to do and requires considerable research and hard work as well as creative inspiration. Once the unique "look" and niche have been found, they must be supported with intelligent marketing. The company should have a name that relates to its niche. Production values should also reflect the theme of the product and its intended quality.

But quality production costs money—substantial money—and this brings us back to the economics of self-publication. It is very difficult to find sufficient initial financing for a self-publication venture (unless you yourself happen to be well-to-do). Quality production is expensive. Per unit economies can generally be achieved only through production in large quantities (requiring more capital). Similarly, it is not possible to achieve distribution by recruiting good sales reps without many different "styles" (distinct cards) in a card line. Having many different styles in a start-up business obviously implies a greater initial investment. Finally, profit margins are low for card publishers. But with all these negatives, starting a self-publishing venture that becomes successful can be done. To do so one must have discipline, vision and perseverance.

As a practical matter, the self-publisher cannot profitably produce fewer initial styles than fit on a printing flat. This is because of technical production requirements; to do otherwise would be wasteful. (See also Chapter 3, *The Print Reproduction Process from A to Z* and the illustration on page 34, depicting a flat of cards.) In normal circumstances, this means eight to twelve different cards. The minimum economically viable press run size for such a flat would be about 3,000 finished sheets (i.e., 24,000 to 36,000 cards), with a cost of between $5,000.00 and $10,000.00.

While a single flat minimum size press run such as the one described above can be done, distribution of so few different cards would be difficult. With pluck and fortitude, doing much of the work oneself, it has on occasion been done. But a more realistic minimum number of styles in order to achieve distribution is one hundred. The initial printing costs to produce 100 different styles in 3,000 unit quantities would be more like $50,000.00 to $100,000.00.

Another reason that self-publishers must produce quite a few different styles initially is that it is a certainty that not all product published will be successful. The winning strategy is to publish enough different styles so that those with sales in the lower 50% can be dropped. No matter who you are, not all your cards will be winners. To create a successful line with a back list, the publisher must be able to stick with the winners and drop the styles that do not do so well.

In our example, let us say that Sally Start-up Self-publishing Company has produced 3,000 units of each of ten different styles of cards for $8,000.00. To calculate per unit cost, divide the toal cost by the quantity printed times number of different styles on the flat.

$$Unit\ Cost = \frac{Total\ Cost}{Quantity\ Printed * Number\ of\ Styles}$$

Let us plug Sally Start-Up's numbers (Total Cost = $8,000, Quantity Printed = 3000, Number of Styles = 10) into this equation:

$$Unit\ Cost = \frac{8,000}{3,000 * 10}$$

Doing the arithmetic in this equation, Unit Cost = $0.27. Sally has produced 30,000 cards for $8,000.00, and her direct per-unit cost is $0.27 (8,000 divided by 30,000). As we shall see in a moment, it is difficult to achieve profitability with unit costs this high.

Let us suppose each card retails for $1.50. ($1.50 represents a reasonably typical retail price for a quality card. But research this. Go to stores and find out how much cards cost. See if you can identify characteristics that seem to justify lesser or greater retail prices.) Stores in the United States purchase inventory using what is known as the keystone markup system. The theory of the keystone markup system is that each business through whose hands inventory passes expects to sell the product for twice what it paid for it. The card store buys the card for $0.75, or half the retail price. This is also known as wholesale. Generally, however, stores will not pay for the cards when they are delivered but expect to be offered "terms," meaning the right to pay the bill at some point after the goods have been delivered.

Standard industry terms are "Net 30 Days," meaning the bill is due in thirty days. But, as a practical matter, often stores will take longer to pay, and some (incredible as this may seem to you!) will never pay at all.

The first deduction from the $0.75 gross

receipt per card is a bad debt allowance and interest on the amount billed (called "receivables"). Let us say $0.02.

Next, we must subtract the sales commission. Independent sales reps for self-publishers generally receive 20% of the amount of the sale, or, in this case, $0.15 per card.

Let us allow the following costs per card: Envelopes, $0.05; Packing and Shipping, $0.10; Invoicing, Accounting and Sales Reps Statements, $0.05. We are now down to a gross receipt of $0.38 per card.

As we noted above, not all cards will sell well. From the 30,000 cards in this hypothetical press run, a proportional allowance must be subtracted for those that don't sell. Let us say that of the ten styles, three are not so successful and only sell half their run (or 1,500 units). (As a practical matter, this is so low an unsalable inventory adjustment as to be unrealistic.) This means that 4,500 cards, at a unit cost of $0.27, for a total cost of $1215.00, are worthless. Their cost must be allocated back as part of the cost of each successful card. In our example, there are 25,500 marketable cards. Each must be charged about $0.05 to cover the pro-rata costs of the unsuccessful inventory, bringing our receipts per card to $0.33.

From our gross profits of $0.33 per card must be subtracted not only the unit cost of $0.27 but also salaries, rent and the cost of capital. It is also important to note that yet to be subtracted are any royalties or fees paid for the use of art or salary to principals. Sally Start-Up's net per unit profit is calculated by first determining the gross profit. In our example above, this is as follows:

$0.75 (Wholesale Price)
$0.02 (Bad Debt Allowance)
$0.15 (Sales Commission)
$0.05 (Envelopes)
$0.10 (Packing and Shipping)
$0.05 (Bookkeeping Costs)
$0.05 (Unsalable Inventory Allowance)
— $0.27 (Direct Production Costs)

$0.06 (Gross Profits)

To calculate net profit, subtract a per unit allocation of salaries, rent, cost of capital and royalties or fees for the use of art from the gross profits (in our example $0.06 per card).

What can be done to improve this unsatisfactory profit margin picture? The simplest and most obvious answer is to produce cards in larger quantities since unit costs go down with larger press runs. But this requires more initial investment. It also increases the quantity of unsalable inventory you will have.

Another step is to do as much work as possible yourself. For example, as Alan Batt, owner of the successful Piece of the Rainbow Cards explains, "Because I am both my own salesperson and artist, I pay neither sales commissions nor royalties."

However, it can be dangerous to attempt to do too much yourself unless you are truly qualified for the roles. Alan Batt can be the leading sales rep for Piece of the Rainbow because he came from a background as a highly successful sales rep before starting his own company. Be selective in what functions you decide to perform. Remember that there is a real cost—even if it is only in your time.

The most effective approach to profit margins is to attempt to add value to the product. Manufacturers of many kinds of consumer goods have long realized that one way to achieve greater profitability is to provide added value service or styling. For example, it costs relatively little more to make a stereo that is cased in a space age well-designed cabinet. Yet such a stereo can sell for much more than one with the same audio specifications housed in a plain case. This approach works very well with cards since, as discussed at the beginning of this section, most of what is being marketed is design and style. The market will pay substantially more for cards that are designed with value added features. The increase in production cost is relatively small compared with the increased wholesale price. A good example of a self-publisher who has successfully employed value adding in his production is Jeff Milstein. His Paper House Productions line of die-cut cards are profiled at the end of this chapter. Other possible examples of value added design include cards that are oversize or that fold or pop out. (But if you design a card of an unusual size, be sure to consider postal regulations and how the card will fit in racks.)

There are many more possibilities. It is up to you as a new self-publisher to come up with a new idea. One thing is clear: in the greeting card market, good designs that are distinctive and produced sell well.

THE ROLE OF THE INDEPENDENT SALES REPRESENTATIVE

The independent sales representative, also called a sales rep or a manufacturer's rep, forms an absolutely crucial part of the distribution chain for a small card publishing company. Sales reps take the publisher's product on the road and sell it to the stores. They are also responsible for servicing accounts. Reps form an integral part of the distribution system in the greeting card industry.

Sales reps, who are usually assured of an exclusive geographic territory, are paid by the publisher with a commission on sales, the terms and amount of which are negotiated in advance with the publisher. Industry standard is 15% to 20% of the amount of the sale. For small card companies, it will usually be 20%.

When the sales rep is paid is also subject to negotiation, but the only arrangement that makes any sense from the point of view of the publisher is to pay the sales reps after the publisher has been paid by the store. That way, the rep has an interest in getting his accounts to pay their bills. (The alternative is payment to the rep when the order is "written." Not only does this place unnecessary demands on the publisher's cash flow, but it also removes the rep's incentive for encouraging timely payments by accounts.)

The goal of the small card publisher is to get a good sales rep covering each territory in the entire country.

Finding and keeping good independent sales representatives is of absolutely crucial importance for independent card publishers. Without goods reps there are no sales and, ultimately, no card company. Sales reps will not carry more than a dozen or so product lines at once, if for no other reason than that they cannot physically carry more "decks" (the term "deck" is used to describe a line of cards published by a given company placed in a deck and held together with a rubber band). Also, an attempt to show more than a few decks at one time will produce glazed boredom on the part of store buyers. Each deck the sales rep carries must produce sales, or the rep will simply stop showing it. A good sales rep will not take on a product line he does not think he can profitably show. Generally, to be worth a good professional rep's while, a deck must contain a <u>minimum</u> of about 50 different styles. This is an important number for the would-be small artist/publisher to keep in mind because it bears on initial start-up capital requirements as discussed in the preceding section.

The reader will observe that being a good independent sales rep is an activity that is

Above: *Porsche Card,* © 1992 AGC, Inc. Reproduced with the permission of American Greetings Corporation. The card is part of American Greeting's CreataCard program, a computerized system that allows consumers to design, personalize and manufacture their own cards.

Right: *Son on His Birthday,* gouache, © 1992 AGC, Inc. Reproduced with the permission of American Greetings Corporation.

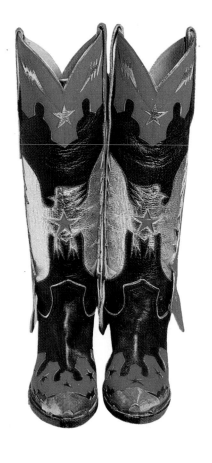

Above: *Common Sunflower,* photograph by Jeff Milstein, © Paper House Productions.

Left: *Cowboy Boots,* photograph by Jeff Milstein, © Paper House Productions.

Below: *1957 Ford Thunderbird,* photograph by Jeff Milstein, © Paper House Productions.

Top: *Pansy,* design by Dorothy Maienschein, ©
Hallmark Cards, Inc. This card has sold over
twenty-seven million copies, since its introduction in 1939. According to Hallmark, it is America's best-selling greeting card.

Bottom: *Three Little Angels Adorn Christmas,*
design by Ruth J. Morehead, © 1977 Hallmark
Cards, Inc. This is Hallmark's all-time, best-selling Christmas card. About twenty million copies have been sold since its introduction.

Left: *Rowboat in Maine,* photograph by Harold Davis, © 1989 Harold Davis, courtesy Wilderness Studio, Inc.

Below: *Chair in Vermont,* photograph by Harold Davis, © 1989 Harold Davis, courtesy Wilderness Studio, Inc.

~ The Dance of Spring is the Dance of Life ~

Denali, The Great One, Alaska · Harold Davis

Top: *Dance of Spring,* photograph by Harold Davis, © 1983 Harold Davis, courtesy Wilderness Studio, Inc.

Bottom: *Denali, The Great One, Alaska,* photograph by Harold Davis, © 1983 Harold Davis, courtesy Wilderness Studio, Inc.

Above Left: *Plum,* watercolor by Yuriko Takata, © 1991 Yuriko Takata, courtesy Bruce McGaw Graphics, Inc.

Above Right: *Rhythm,* design by Ty Wilson, © 1987 Ty Wilson, courtesy Bruce McGaw Graphics, Inc.

Left: *Little Angels,* photograph by Betsy Cameron, © 1992 Betsy Cameron, courtesy Bruce McGaw Graphics, Inc.

Top: *View from 'La Route des Cretes',* painting by John Stockwell, © 1991 by John Stockwell, courtesy Bruce McGaw Graphics, Inc.

Bottom: *Patrick's Porch,* painting by Alice Dalton Brown, © 1988 Alice Dalton Brown, courtesy Bruce McGaw Graphics, Inc.

Top: *Blue Stair and Begonias,* watercolor by John Atwater, © 1988 New York Graphic Society, Ltd.

Bottom: *Garden for Master Proust,* oil by Piet Bekaert, © 1993 New York Graphic Society, Ltd.

essentially entrepreneurial in nature. (It is also highly physical, since it involves lugging decks of card samples from store to store.) An impact of this is that over time the better sales reps form repping organizations. Generally, the founder of a repping organization receives a portion of the sales commissions that each of his sub-reps makes. This way, the organization can cover a much broader territory than any single individual could. Also, fledgling sales reps can learn from the experience of the founder of the organization. Possibly, also, the repping organization will maintain a showroom and a presence at industry trade shows.

Initially, the best way to find sales reps is through word of mouth. Card store buyers will have strong opinions about them and can refer you to several sales reps if they are so inclined. There is a kind of rep network as well: the good sales reps tend to know each other. Your rep for one territory will refer you to reps in other territories.

Trade shows are also a good place to find reps. Some will come to you if you have a booth, but, if you don't, many trade shows have a Reps Wanted/Reps Available bulletin board. You will also find related advertising in the classified section of *Greetings*.

Ultimately, card companies with lines that are profitable to their sales reps can attract the highest caliber of people. To keep relationships with productive reps, communication must be kept open. Discuss concerns and find out at once the reason for a marked sales decline in a particular territory. Be prompt about sending your reps money and statements they are due.

While sales reps by nature of the profession can come and go, if you treat them following the precepts of the golden rule and inculcate the sense that they are part of your extended family, you are more likely to build a sales network that will last.

INTERVIEW WITH
JEFF MILSTEIN OF
PAPER HOUSE PRODUCTIONS

Jeff Milstein's Paper House Productions is a thriving niche card publishing company. The company's signature cutout cards depict diverse subject matter such as classic cars, flowers, animals, Victorian houses, and characters from *The Wizard of Oz*. (See reproductions of some Paper House Production cards on page 82.)

The Paper House format has been widely imitated but never equaled. Many designs use the artistic and model-making talents of company founder and owner Jeff Milstein who was trained as an architect and photographer. His cards have received many awards for design. The company is successful enough to support an average of ten employees, a warehousing and distribution facility, and a state-of-the-art studio complex.

Milstein's spacious working studio and design center is located outside Woodstock, New York. There are facilities for table-top photography, photographic print making and model making. In addition, Paper House has invested heavily in desktop publishing work stations and image manipulation applications such as PhotoShop. The studio contains an eclectic collection of things besides artistic tools. A jukebox is positioned to one side of the front door. Milstein's scale models of antique toys and classic houses line many shelves.

Milstein states, "I spend two-thirds of my time running the business and one third doing creative things. I wish the proportion were reversed. There is just not enough time for my creative projects."

He grew up in West Los Angeles the ,"... kind of kid whose paintings hung on the Kindergarten walls. I always felt that I would have a career in the fine arts or perhaps advertising. Instead, I went to architecture school at Berkeley—and also pursued photography. After graduating, I took a job with a small creative architecture firm in New York. *Family Circle* commissioned me to build a small country home. The house was the basis for a story which included its architectural plans. This is what got me to the Woodstock area, and I just stayed. *Family Circle* also commissioned a build-it-yourself doll house using recycled corrugated. This idea later turned into a book of five classic American house designs using recycled corrugate, with history les-sons about the designs. Unfortunately, the publisher never promoted the book, and it dropped out of sight. They took my completed project, said 'Thank you,' and I never heard from them again. Some publishers, I have found, just do not know how to market things. This is partly what led me to become my own publisher. But, of course, absolute control is also a headache. Anyhow, I got the rights back to the doll house designs book, used my savings, and published a flat of cards. The flat consisted of six card designs. Each was a die cut version of a classic American house design, for example, Victorian and Greek revival. Each card—and this is part of our formula to this day—had a descriptive text and history lesson on the back. Originally, I wrote these. Now, I sometimes use professional writers, particularly on cards that call for technical information.

"I found a few sales reps by word of mouth. I asked store owners who sold them their cards. There is a kind of sales rep network. One sales rep referred me to reps in other territories.

"These sales reps helped me sell those first cards until I had enough money to publish another flat of six architectural cards. But then, the reps started saying to me, 'This is fine—but what are you going to do next?'"

Today, Paper House Productions has over 250 different die cut card styles. Besides Victorian houses, subject matter includes domestic and wild animals, sea creatures, flowers, food, and "planes, trains and automobiles."

"We have a high class niche," states Milstein. "Our product has an excellent reputation with many better stores. We have a loyal following. I really don't want to sell to schlocky stores."

Paper House Productions is essentially a vehicle for Milstein's creative ideas. Coping with business issues such as fulfillment, collections and inventory control is the price he must pay—one he feels is well worth it—to keep the vehicle going. Milstein is low key and essentially modest about his accomplishments. But the truth is that he has achieved remarkable success as a self-publishing artist. He is also in the position of having created an extensive functioning design studio which he can now use to empower his vision as he sees fit.

While Milstein does buy some art directly from photographers and also works with stock agencies, he prefers to use his own photographs. As he puts it, "I do all the tabletop of things that won't eat me for lunch." Many of his photographs are used in the best selling Paper House cards. For example, he photographed the ruby slippers used by Judy Garland in *The Wizard of Oz*. (Paper House licensed the right to

do an Oz series from Turner Entertainment.) And, Milstein's photographs of flowers are perennial company best sellers.

What next? "My experience," he states, "is that I do things, people copy them, and then I move on. In this business, one must always keep inventing. There are many smaller companies out there doing wonderful work. Generally, they are staying on the creative edge. They keep inventing. To get a chance to do this and see one's ideas carried out is such a thrill.

"Right now, I'm very excited about using computers and high-end desk top publishing to push the edge. We have quality staff in this area. We are looking to use the new technologies to produce creative and unusual paper products and related gift items."

■

Starting a card publishing business should only be undertaken with realism regarding low profit margins in the card industry and difficulty in arranging for distribution. However, success stories such as those of Jeff Milstein and others indicate that individuals who possess both artistic vision and business acumen can create self-publishing enterprises that reward them both financially and creatively. ◆

8.

How to Find a Fine Art Poster Publisher

As opposed to the greeting card industry, fine art posters are distributed in a centralized fashion. This works both to the advantage and disadvantage of the artist. While there is no need to establish one's own distribution network, distribution is controlled by a few powerful companies. Further discussion of the implications of this for the artist will be found in this and the next chapter.

Posters are also a product with a considerably higher retail price—and per-unit profit—than cards. But they lack the broad consumer saturation of the greeting card industry. An art poster is not a disposable item. Once it is framed and put on a wall it is likely to stay there for some time. This is a very different situation—with important implications for the artist—than in the greeting card industry where the primary intent of the consumer is to mail or give away his purchase.

This chapter gives an introduction to the

fine art poster industry and describes the workings of publishers as related to the acquisition of art. Information is provided to help guide artists who are submitting work to publishers and for those who may need information about customary business practices in the industry.

THE FINE ART POSTER INDUSTRY

"Our industry is closely related to certain other industries," states Martin B. Lawlor, Director of Purchasing for Bruce McGaw Graphics, Inc., a leading fine art poster publishing company. "The latest trends in interior design and home furnishing are almost certain to be reflected in the art poster business."

Fine art posters are found primarily on walls in homes and as institutional decor. Consumers, whether corporate or individual, purchase them from art galleries, framing shops, interior decorators, and corporate art consultants. These middle men obtain them at wholesale from publishing companies such as Bruce McGaw Graphics, Graphique de France, and New York Graphic Society. There are fewer than a dozen major fine art poster publishing companies in the United States. Most poster publishing companies also function as <u>distributors</u> of posters that have been independently produced by artists or their representatives. The next chapter will examine how this distribution mechanism works; this chapter will be concerned only with the major publishers in their role as <u>publishers</u>.

The publishers generally maintain showrooms and a sales force. More important, they publish and distribute to the art trade massive and lavish catalogs. These catalogs generate the vast bulk of fine art poster sales. Besides sales through graphics galleries and framing shops—which put the catalogs on display so that consumers can order any poster that is not in the retailer's inventory—decorators, designers, corporate art consultants, and architects use the catalogs as sales reference material to show clients.

What makes a fine art poster successful? See the discussion in Chapter 2, *Imagery that Works*. Good design and strong production values are both extremely important. In terms of the art that appears as part of the poster, there are two approaches that seem to work. One is to use the poster as a vehicle for the reproduction of "classical" art. Paintings by the French impressionist, Claude Monet, are the subject matter of the most successful reproduction posters.

Posters that are vehicles for contemporary art tend to succeed when the art is decorative, cheerful and moderately subtle. It helps if the art "works" with colors that are in vogue in the interior design and home furnishing industries. The importance of appropriate integration of design with art cannot be overemphasized. Many posters are purchased to provide color and something escapist to look at for offices or similar institutional areas. Imagery, such as nature photographs, that takes the viewer away from reality towards an idealized or apparently better place, can be very successful. Controversial imagery, political imagery, imagery that depicts squalor, and explicitly sexual imagery do not generally work as fine art posters.

Within these general parameters, a very wide variety of high quality imagery has succeeded as poster art.

The artist should realize that there is no job more important to the poster publishing companies than finding, and obtaining the rights to use, art that is appropriate for publication. Without new posters to publish, these companies are in deep trouble. It is, however, a surprisingly difficult job. A great deal of work is submitted "over the transom" to fine art poster publishing companies. Much of it is inappropriate for the market or just won't work for reasons that are difficult to pin down. To succeed in discovering new sources of poster art, the publishing companies must establish procedures that efficiently winnow out the submissions that are genuine possibilities for publication. Generally, fine art poster publishing companies do not have huge staffs. Unsolicited submissions—while necessary to the continuation of the industry—can be a considerable nuisance to publishers. Most publishers have talented and dedicated professionals who handle unsolicited submissions. Generally, the same people will also be in charge of acquiring art by established artists. Typically, those in charge of acquisitions will have some background in fine art as well as in business. It is normal for this acquisitions staff to refer major decisions to a standing committee to get a broad consensus of opinions. Final decisions are usually made by the owner of the publishing business.

As noted above, few decisions are as important to fine art publishers as those involved in finding and publishing successful pieces. In light of this, acquisitions staffs at the publishers have become very good at their job. While they cannot predict with certainty what the sales will be for any given piece, generally they can fairly accurately assess prospects at an early stage. To help acquisitions staff make these decisions, it has become common for publishers to produce "comps" of pieces they are seriously considering. (A "comp," short for "comprehensive dummy," is a term, borrowed from the book industry, which means an accurate mock-up, usually in reduced scale; see Chapter 4, *Creating a Design for Publication*.) In the fine art poster industry, the comp includes design elements as well as a reproduction (probably photographic) of the art. The comp is displayed to the publisher's important customers, such as the buyers for chain art galleries such as Decor, Deck the Walls, and Prints Plus. Responses from the buyer helps the publishers in their decision-making process.

A crucial number for the publisher is the "break-even point." This means, how many copies of a piece must the publisher sell before he has made back his costs? The larger the break-even point, the greater the risk to the publisher.

Calculating break-even points is complex and depends on many variables. The most significant of these variables are the cost of acquiring the art and the cost of production. Except with very popular artists, who have considerable negotiating clout, publishers usually can acquire art on a royalty basis with little or no advance payments. By lowering up-front payments, they are lowering their break-even point, and are therefore reducing the risk of investing in a particular piece.

The cost of production primarily includes the cost of separations, printing and paper (see Chapter 3, *The Print Reproduction Process from A to Z*). These will vary substantially depending on the size of the publisher, the volume of purchases, and the publisher's relationship with the vendor.

A range of plausible break-even points in the fine art poster industry would be from 300 to 1,000 copies. Sales over the break-even point are almost entirely profitable to the publisher. As a consequence, while publishers are usually reluctant to make significant advances, they are often prepared to pay substantial royalties (see the discussion of royalties later in this chapter), particularly after production expenses have been recouped.

PROMOTIONAL CONSIDERATIONS

For an artist, having a well-designed poster published is a major professional achievement apart from any direct economic benefit.   It is a tremendously significant showcase for the artist's work. Exhibitions of an artist's work come down usually in a month or so. Often the work is then forgotten and relegated to storage in the artist's studio. But a poster, on the other hand, has the possibility of lasting a very long time. In addition, the very act of the publication of a poster is an implied endorsement of the worth and commercial viability of the artist. The poster will be placed in catalogs directed to art galleries nationally and possibly promoted in the art trade press.

Generally, fine art poster publishers do a superb job of design and printing. Their reproduction standards are high, as they must be in order to create salable fine art poster inventory. The context of the poster states, "The work reproduced herein is significant!"

For these reasons, a nationally published fine art poster is the best calling card an artist can have. Artists can use the posters in any number of helpful promotional ways. For example, a signed poster makes a prestigious gift to an art dealer who is considering handling one's original work. In addition, posters, signed and unsigned, can be sold at exhibitions or through the artist's studio.

It is therefore important that artists make sure to negotiate beforehand to receive complimentary copies of the finished piece for their own use. Generally, it is standard in the industry for the artist to receive 50-100 complimentary copies. A discounted purchase price, in case the artist needs more copies than the complimentary allowance, should also be negotiated in advance. The discounted price should be the wholesale price or less.

To the extent that posters of an artist's work are successful, there will be great additional impact on the artist's career. Visually literate people, including gallery owners, art dealers, designers, and others, will be familiar with successful posters. They will pay attention to the artists whose works have been reproduced as posters. They are more likely to consider exhibiting or marketing originals or prints made by successful poster artists. Quite a few artists who have successful careers today credit the publication of posters of their work as the break that gave them their start. Apart from the royalties they have received—which can be quite substantial—these artists remember their initial interaction with fine art poster publishers with gratitude as having jump-started their careers.

HOW TO SUBMIT WORK TO AN ART POSTER PUBLISHER

The late Paul J. Liptak, formerly Director of Acquisitions for Bruce McGaw Graphics, commented, "Much of the work that is submitted to us is beautiful but not appropriate for our market. Artists should study our sales material. We would like to publish all the quality work that is submitted to us, but, of course, we cannot. Professional artists accept rejection with grace and persist to find a publisher appropriate for their work."

Vertical and horizontal imagery works equally well in the fine art poster market.

First, contact the publisher and find out to whom submissions should be addressed. Then, make an attractive presentation that does not include any originals. A sheet of twenty duplicate slides is best. Label each slide with your name and a title. An elaborate cover letter is unnecessary, but a short biographical statement may be helpful.

For further information on the form of a submission, review the suggestions in the section "Making a Submission" in Chapter 6, *How to Find Greeting Card Publishers for your Work.*

"Imagery should speak for itself," continues the Director of Acquisitions quoted above. "We do not particularly like, and do not feel it helps the artist's cause, when an artist tries to sell his work."

HOW TO GIVE YOUR WORK THE BEST CHANCE FOR PUBLICATION

While quality work sells itself—despite the strenuous efforts of some artists to sabotage their sales through inappropriate pushiness—there are several steps you can take to give your work the best chance for publication.

It is very helpful to regard the process of selling your work as distinct from the process of creating it. This is the technique that I have termed wearing a "different hat." Try to place some emotional distance between yourself and your work. However it may feel, you are not your work, and a rejection of your work is not a rejection of you. Notes one publisher, "Even if it were all good, one simply could not publish everything that came along. There have to be some, 'Nos.' Professional artists take rejections gracefully without making a scene."

It can be inferred that this publisher has left unsaid his discomfort with telling artists, "No." Artists who make the sometimes inevitable process of rejection—and it is inevitable sometimes, even for famous artists—socially palatable to publishers by making it clear that they do not take it personally may well live to be published by the rejecter on another day.

Besides not taking rejection personally, it is helpful to seem professional without being pushy. Acquisitions staff will react positively and with flexibility to artists who project an attitude of relaxed professionalism.

Attempt to research needs of the publishers so that you can present them with exactly what they want. Artist Betsy Cameron attended a seminar given by the staff of Bruce McGaw Graphics at a trade show. During the question and answer period, Cameron raised her hand and asked what subject matter currently was most wanted by the publisher. Based on this information, Cameron presented a portfolio consisting of her hand colored photographs of children. Her pieces have been among the best sellers at McGaw for over five years. Notes one McGaw staffer, "Cameron's work is nostalgic but contemporary, romantic but innocent. The sales of her posters, particularly *Two Children on the Beach*, have been amazing. People buy these for the beach house and for kids' rooms.

"When Cameron first came to us, we passed on her work several times. But she was very persistent: professional, polite and very persistent. We did comps of her work and our customers wanted to pick up her work based on the comps. From that point on her work sold itself with no promotion and no hoopla."

As Betsy Cameron's true-life success story suggests, you can give your work the best chance of publication by taking the time to research the poster industry. This can be done by attending trade shows such as Artexpo, carefully studying the poster inventory in galleries, reading trade publications such as *Decor* and *Art Business News*, and paying attention to poster catalogs.

Whenever you get the chance, listen to the needs of the publishers. Attempt to fulfill these needs. Exhibit professionalism in the presentation of your work and in your own attitude. Persist when rejected, but do so with politeness and courtesy.

CONTRACTUAL TERMS AND ECONOMIC CONSIDERATIONS

Each publishing company in the fine art poster industry has its own way of doing business. The standard contractual terms that artists are offered vary from company to company. Key financial provisions of these contracts are probably not negotiable except by artists with a significant track record. However, it is a truism that the time to examine and question the terms of a contract is before the contract is signed, not after. A written contract is merely an offer of terms until it is signed and accepted. Once the contract has been accepted, it is too late to negotiate.

There are several common financial arrangements regarding payment to artists for use of their work as posters. They are:

(1) Payment of a royalty per poster sold. The royalty can be expressed as a percentage of the retail price, the wholesale price, or of actual receipts to the publisher. Generally, this royalty will amount to between $0.25 and $0.50 per piece. A non-refundable advance against sales may be paid to the artist at the time the contract is signed.

(2) Payment of a royalty on sales after the publisher has recouped production expenses. Generally, this royalty is substantial, perhaps 10% of the publisher's sales. As will be discussed below, there are some drawbacks to this scheme from the artist's point of view, including the fact that it may be quite a while before the artist receives any income from the poster.

(3) Payment of a flat fee and a specified number of posters for a specified printing run, to be repeated in a pro-rata fashion for subsequent print runs. For example, Paul Publisher might agree to pay Sally Artist $1,000 and 100 posters for each printing run of 3,000 posters. In this example, the monetary fee is equivalent to a royalty of $0.33 per poster, except that it is paid up-front. This arrangement has fallen out of favor with publishers and is more common in the production of multiple prints than it is in the fine art poster industry today.

(4) Payment of a flat one-time fee for unlimited usage of an image as a poster. Generally, the fee offered will be less than $1000.00. This is the one arrangement that the artist should consider turning down out of hand. If the poster sells extremely well, the artist will never see more than this initial fee.

There are some things to be cautious about in a proposed contract in addition to the flat fee buyout. First, be sceptical of arrangements that tie the artist's compensation to production costs. There is absolutely no practical way for an artist to verify production costs.

Royalty arrangements are best when the royalty is specified as a percentage of the retail price rather than another number such as the publisher's net proceeds because retail prices are clear and objective and easier to verify. A payment period for royalties should be specified. For example, royalties could be paid and a statement provided every six months. The artist, or the artist's representatives, should have the right to examine the books of the publisher under reasonable conditions.

Make sure that you understand what rights you are licensing to the publisher. Generally, the publisher should be receiving rights only to reproduce the work as a poster. Other uses should not be included without additional fees applying.

If only a flat one-time fee is being paid, there should be a limit on the period of the license, for example, three years.

The contract should provide that the

copyright to the poster is in the artist's name. The publisher should be required to include a copyright notice on the poster, and possibly, to register the poster in the artist's name with the United States Copyright Office.

The number of complimentary artist's copies should be specified. The price at which the artist may buy additional copies should be stated.

The different kinds of contractual arrangements, and pitfalls described here, may sound daunting. But it is not as bad as it seems. Have a lawyer or business expert who is familiar with the art industry review the contract you are offered, and then discuss it with that person. (It may be helpful to call this chapter to the attention of your advisor.) Generally, there should not be much of a problem resolving any issues with a publisher who is on the level and excited about your work.

While signing the first poster contract may be an anxiety provoking process, the results will be well worth it. Your work is about to be published as a fine art poster! It will be distributed nationally, and maybe internationally, to galleries and art dealers! Once you have a track record and a relationship within the industry, subsequent projects should not present as many hurdles. Perhaps many of your images will become posters. It is not unlikely that some day you will be somewhere—in an office, a motel room, a home, a store—and see your poster on the wall. What a thrill! ◆

9.

Self-Publishing and Distributing Art Posters

*I*t is easy to obtain centralized distribution for a marketable product in the fine art poster industry. This fact makes self-publication of fine art posters a very real possibility for the artist. Every artist who is involved or would like to be involved with the fine art poster industry should at least consider self-publishing. There are no barriers to stop an artist who can design marketable fine art posters and is willing to financially back them from maintaining control of his work and reaping the full financial rewards from his work's success.

A CLOSER LOOK AT THE STRUCTURE AND ECONOMICS OF THE INDUSTRY

As we have seen, the art poster industry is dominated by a handful of companies that function as both publishers and distributors. (To review the distinction, a publisher creates, designs, produces and markets a poster. A distributor merely buys the poster and resells it at a higher price.) The only significant distribution channel in the fine art poster industry is through placement in the catalogs produced by these distribution and publication companies.

The publication and distribution companies would always rather publish than merely distribute a <u>successful</u> poster because their per unit profits are higher on a product they have published. On distributed product they make only the keystone markup; if they have published the poster, they make the profit on publishing <u>plus</u> the keystone markup. Conversely, there is less risk in distributing than in publishing a poster because the company lays out money to purchase only small quantities of inventory as opposed to putting up greater sums to purchase the larger amounts of inventory required to publish a poster. The buyers can take more chances on distributed material because the risk is not as great.

Many of the industry's more successful fine art posters are published by independents. My company, Wilderness Studio, discussed in the introductory chapter of *Publishing Your Art As Cards, Posters & Calendars*, is an example of an independent publishing company; there are quite a few other examples of self-publishing companies founded as vehicles for their work by successful poster artists.

Each of the major distribution companies feels compelled to distribute—or, as it is sometimes termed, "catalog"—enough of the successful independent pieces to keep its overall product mix desirable and interesting.

Generally, distributors sell posters to retailers for 50% of the retail price. In turn, they purchase posters from independents for 25% of the retail price. This is known in the trade as "50% of 50". For example, let us suppose Jane Artist produces a $25.00 retail poster. She sells it to the distributor for $6.25. The distributor sells it to a graphics gallery for $12.50 who sells it to the end consumer for $25.00. Jane Artist's unit gross profit (e.g., profit not considering cost of capital and salaries) is the difference between production costs plus attributable overhead and $6.25. In recent years, there has been pressure to discount more at all levels of this pricing structure, leading to sales by some independents at prices such as 50% of 50 less 20%. (In our example this works out to a unit price to Jane Artist of $5.00.)

While this pricing structure may seem at first glance not to be fair to the independent producer, in fact it compares favorably with the reality of profit margins in many manufacturing industries. There is a sufficient per unit profit potential in the fine art poster industry to justify either a substantial royalty to the artist who works directly with a publisher or the investment of capital to produce his own posters for resale under the right circumstances.

Let us look at the economics of our example more closely from Jane Artist's point of view. A quality poster today retails for between $25.00 and $35.00. Let us suppose that Jane Artist has published "My Poster" and established a retail price of $30.00. The normal 50% of 50 price to distributors for "My Poster" would then be $7.50 each. The usual minimum order from a distributor is twenty-five pieces.

Some distributors who buy "My Poster" from Jane Artist have negotiated a better price and are paying her only 50% of 50 less 20%, or $6.00 per poster. In partial exchange for the reduced price, Jane Artist has received improved payment terms (these distributors pay her when they place the order) and has established minimum quantity requirements of 100 pieces.

To summarize the receipts side of Jane Artist's business selling "My Poster," she is getting between $6.00 and $7.50 (an average of $6.75) per poster based on orders of between 25 and 100 pieces. Payment terms are in advance or on a net 30-day basis. To make a sound business decision whether to publish "My Poster," Jane needs to know what her unit cost is and how many posters she must sell before she breaks even.

Many important factors go into calculating production expenses, including most run size, the choice of printer, the paper stock selected, and the presence or absence of expensive design elements. Readers are referred to Chapters 3 through 5 of this book for a detailed discussion of these issues.

For the sake of our example, let us say that Jane Artist printed 3,000 copies of "My Poster" at a total direct cost of $6,000.00, resulting in a unit cost of $2.00. "My Poster" is well produced and well designed. It measures 25" X 36". Eighty pound ("80lb.") premium dull coated cover stock has been used. The art is handsome and looks good. This oversized poster seems like a winner.

Jane Artist knows that had she printed 5,000 pieces, the cost would have been $7,500.00, for a unit cost of $1.50. 10,000 copies would have cost $10,000.00, for a $1.00 unit cost. But Ms. Artist has no certainty about how many copies she will sell. If "My Poster" turns out to be a hit, she will reprint in larger quantities, bringing down her per unit cost. (Since she will not have to remake her separations, reprint costs will be lower anyhow, even if she were only producing the same quantity as the first

press run.) For the time being, $6000.00 is all the money that she can prudently risk. She forgoes the lower per unit cost that a higher volume press run would bring in exchange for minimizing her risk.

Jane Artist's direct production costs on "My Poster" are $6,000. Her average per-unit receipt is $6.75. This means that her break-even point is 889 copies. ($6000.00 divided by $6.75 equals 889.)

It is likely that "My Poster" will either sell very few copies (much fewer than the 889 copies Jane needs to break even) or a great many copies (substantially more than the 889 that Jane needs to make back her direct production costs). This reflects the reality of the fine art poster business: there are few partial successes. Pieces either flop, or they succeed.

Even if "My Poster" is a hit, it may take a while to sell those first 889 copies. Cataloging—when a distributor adds a poster to their catalog—occurs at the convenience of the distribution company, not at the convenience of the producer. It may be months before distributors have picked the piece up. Initial orders can be small. Jane Artist must be resigned to wait a minimum of six months before making back her investment even if "My Poster" will ultimately be a success.

Let us look at the unit profitability of "My Poster." From the average per unit receipt of $6.75, subtract direct production costs of $2.00. Next, subtract return for damage allocation of $0.675 (see below). If warehousing and fulfillment are contracted out, the cost per unit is about $0.75. (See the section on "Fulfillment" later in this chapter.) We are thus left with a per unit profit of $3.325. (This figure is, of course, gross profit. It does not include cost of capital, rent, salaries, or payment of fees or royalties for art.)

One constant in the fine art poster industry is the return to the vendor of any poster that shows even minor flaws such as creases or wrinkles. This figure can run as high as 10% of the quantity shipped, and the goods returned must be destroyed. (This is not the same as the "returns allowance" that book publishers must allocate against the contingency of returns of unsold books from stores, but it is still a very real cost. It is known as, "return for damage allocation.")

Based on the per unit profit figure of $3.325, should Jane Artist sell her entire run of 3,000 posters, she would have made a profit of $9750.00 in addition to recouping her original investment of $6,000.00. (The costs of producing "My Poster" were recouped from Jane's per unit average gross receipts of $6.75, not the $3.325 which represents pure profit.) Obviously, in this case, Jane should plan to celebrate by inviting all her artist friends to a big party. Jane has more than doubled her money. But, before she spends it all on that big artist's bash, she must be sure to put aside money to pay for the next printing of "My Poster."

The conclusion is clear that for the artist who knows what she is doing, substantial money can be made in self-publishing posters. No royalty arrangement could ever have provided Jane the money she made by self-publishing and selling the entire first press run of "My Poster." Jane certainly did well with self-publishing. But Jane knew that self-publishing was not for those with weak stomachs. She could easily have lost her entire investment.

From the artist's point of view, one great virtue of self-publishing posters is the extent to which the business can be streamlined. If warehousing and fulfillment is contracted out, once the posters have been published, the artist does little more than process orders from time to time. This means that the artist can have enough time to continue producing new work.

GETTING DISTRIBUTION

It is best to have at least one piece produced by a major publishing company before attempting to self-publish. There are several reasons for this. First, a successful publication of your work by a prestigious publishing company functions as certification of the marketability of your work. Buyers at the distribution companies are more likely to take your self-published pieces seriously if they are already familiar with your conventionally published poster. Second, publishers know what they are doing. If none of them will publish an initial piece of yours, perhaps you should reconsider before sinking your cash into the project.

Furthermore, the industry contacts you will make through getting your first poster published will help you sell subsequent self-published pieces.

Decisions on cataloging independent posters may be made by the same people who make acquisitions decisions, or there may be others who make these decisions with titles such as "Director of Purchasing." A phone call to the distributor will indicate to whom poster samples should be sent.

Poster distributors take the decision to catalog extremely seriously. For one thing, each poster reproduced in the catalog represents a substantial investment. For another, the catalog represents the company. The product mix it contains will determine the success or the failure of the distributor.

Almost without exception, distributors will not make a final decision to catalog a poster based on anything but the final produced piece. It is still a good idea to meet with any buyers who will see you and present a good comp (see Chapter 4, *Creating a Design for Publication* for a discussion of comps) before finalizing your design and production decisions. The feedback of the buyers—they know what sells—is very valuable. Also, if they have seen a project in an early stage—and played some role in shaping its direction—they will take more interest in it when it is time to decide whether to catalog it.

Finished poster samples should be delivered without wrinkles or creases. Where feasible they should be hand delivered or sent via FedEx. A simple informative sheet should accompany the posters. It should include: your company name, contact name, address and phone; the title(s) and dimension(s) of the poster(s), and the retail price(s).

It is perfectly possible for samples to get lost in the shuffle. You should place a polite call to the buyer a few weeks after he should have received your samples to make sure they arrived.

FULFILLMENT

Fulfillment is a term that means the warehousing of inventory and its shipment to customers. Fulfillment is a particularly critical issue in the fine art poster industry because posters are so fragile and because, as art, they are scrutinized so carefully. Retailers can be expected to return any piece that arrives even the least bit damaged. To protect themselves, the receiving departments at the distribution companies must inspect all incoming shipments carefully and return damaged pieces to the publishers. Generally, common carriers such as UPS will take no responsibility for these damages, even when shipments are insured and the damage appears to be the carrier's fault.

There are only limited options available to the self-publisher. He must make sure that posters are inspected for damage as they come in from the printer. He must make sure they are well packed when they go out. And he must prepare for returns by allocating a percentage of gross receipts as a return allowance. This percentage can average 10-20%. It is vitally important to keep it down by handling fulfillment well.

The self-publishing artist can personally supervise fulfillment or contract with a professional organization for fulfillment services. If the artist handles it personally, he must be prepared to set aside space for warehousing inventory and packing orders. He must also set aside time for learning how to manage inventory, how to pack, packing and waiting for UPS pickups.

Fulfillment services handle all the heavy work and details. Generally, self-publishers fax a shipping order to the fulfillment company who handles the rest.

Fulfillment companies generally charge a monthly rent for warehousing inventory plus a per poster packing fee. (Actual shipping costs are additional, of course.)

Whether to handle fulfillment yourself or contract it out is a personal decision. If you decide to do it yourself, make sure that you have the space, time and inclination for the job. If you decide to contract it, make sure the fulfillment service does its job well. Get references. Inspect the warehouse to make sure your inventory won't get damaged or destroyed. While doing it yourself has costs, consider the bottom line of the fulfillment service charges. Is your self-publishing business still going to be profitable?

■

Self-publishing of fine art posters presents a tremendous opportunity for the artist with appropriate work and an entrepreneurial bent. Some of the psychological and practical issues involved in starting a self-publishing business will be examined in Chapter 11, *A More Detailed Look at the Self-Publishing Option.* ◆

10.

The Calendar Market

It is possible for artists to license their imagery to calendar publishers, to promote (and license for publication) a theme calendar made up entirely of their imagery, or to self-publish a calendar. This chapter explores all three options.

BOOK TRADE DISTRIBUTION

In two important respects, calendars are more like books than they are like cards and posters. First, a calendar is an aggregation of linked and related imagery. It does not stand or fall on one image but instead depends on a collection of imagery. Second, calendars are primarily distributed by book distribution companies. This is because the most important retail sales outlets for calendars are bookstores. (Calendars are also sold in card and variety stores, museum gift shops, and by direct mail.)

Many calendar publishing operations are imprints of book publishing companies. Those that are not subsidiaries of book publishers but are independent entities function in most important respects the way book publishers do. Therefore, artists who wish to work with calendar publishers, or to distribute self-published calendars, would do well to understand the basics of book trade distribution. (Self-publishers of cards should note that distribution to the book trade can be an important secondary market for upper-end cards.)

Retail bookstores buy their inventory in three ways: directly from trade publishers; through wholesalers such as Baker & Taylor and Ingram that function as order consolidators and jobbers for the industry; or through independent distribution companies such as Publishers Group West. A given store may purchase in all three ways or use only one or two of the methods.

The independent distribution companies

function essentially as sales representatives for publishers who are too small to have in-house sales staff. While the distinction between wholesalers and distributors in the book trade may not be totally clear at first glance, it is important and not arcane. Generally, the wholesalers do not take a substantial inventory position in any product and do not care very much if one book sells more than another. In essence, they function as a highly sophisticated computerized way for stores to simplify their buying process by going to one source for all the items they want.

Distributors, on the other hand, are in the business of promoting specific books or calendars. Besides selling these products directly to stores for a commission, they may provide a whole range of services to the (generally small) publishers they represent, including warehousing, fulfilling and cataloging.

Generally, retailers in the book industry purchase inventory at 55% to 60% of retail. This is slightly less of a discount than the keystone markup (50%) that applies in the card and poster industries. The reason for this is that publishers in the book trade must accept, for credit or refund, returns from stores of unsold merchandise. They therefore expect to get a higher profit on the merchandise they sell to compensate for their absorption of the cost of returns. What percentage of the retail price the publisher actually gets, of course, depends on whether the publisher has sold the merchandise directly to the store. If the merchandise has been

obtained through middle organizations—distributors or wholesalers—these organizations must take their cut.

Book publishers generally introduce new products twice a year, in the spring and fall, by publishing a catalog (called a "list" in the book industry). However, with calendars, timing of publication is a critical issue which does not coincide with the usual publication timetables. Calendars for the year 1996 must be in the stores in the autumn of 1995. To make their way through the distribution channels into the stores by September, 1995 calendars must be through production by the end of February, 1995. Artists who wish to license imagery to calendar publishers should note that production schedules often call for image selection from one to two years ahead of production. In our example, the imagery for a 1996 calendar may be decided upon in 1993.

SELLING IMAGERY TO CALENDAR PUBLISHERS

The great advantage of licensing imagery to publishers is that this involves work you already have completed. There is no further outlay of time or money—other than what is required to sell the work. This kind of licensing represents either a secondary use of work created for other purposes or the first use of personal work that has not yet been used. As such, the creative energy is in the past. Usage fees you receive are what is termed "unearned income," meaning there is nothing you have to do in the present to get the money, except, as noted above, to sell your imagery to the publishers.

Actually, this kind of licensing of imagery to calendar publishers, which in the photography world is termed selling "stock," is not terribly difficult or time consuming provided you have appropriate imagery.

While calendars are not expected to have the longevity of the fine art poster—by definition, the use of a calendar is limited to a year —they are expected to contain memorable imagery. Wall calendars must be sufficiently attractive for consumers to want to mount. Desk calendars must be lived with for the entire year.

As with other paper products, the best way to conduct market research on what works as calendar art is to carefully observe as many calendars as possible. This is best done during the peak calendar sales season—autumn—in a bookstore such as one of the larger branches of Barnes and Noble that carries a good selection of calendars.

Imagery on a given calendar is generally attractive, colorful and thematically linked. To be successful, a calendar's theme must appeal to a wide group of people although any particular theme does not have to appeal to everybody. Examples of successful calendar themes include wilderness landscapes (e.g., the hugely suc-

cessful Sierra Club calendars), antique automobiles, quilts, teddy bears, toys, the art of Georgia O'Keefe, motorcycles, and women in swimsuits. While art in almost every media has been successfully used in calendars, it is an area in which photography seems particularly appropriate and has been used far more than any other medium.

The trick to licensing imagery into this market is to study the area and obtain want lists from the major calendar publishers. These want lists, along with the publishers' guidelines for submissions, will give you an idea of the schedules and needs of the publishers. One good source of listings of calendar publishers is the annual calendar issue of *Publishers Weekly* that appears every year sometime in March. Select calendar publishers from whose current publications you would expect to have an affinity with your work. Write to them, requesting guidelines and want lists. Be sure to include an SASE.

When making "stock" submissions to a publisher, be sure to include two copies of a Delivery Memo (see sample provided to the right).

The Delivery Memo includes a total count of the items submitted. One copy is for the publisher to return, acknowledging the count of items received. You must also be sure to make a copy of the Delivery Memo for your files before sending your submission off. Note that in the calendar field, the standard holding provision term in the Delivery Memo limit-

Delivery Memo

DATE

TO: Ms. Terry DuMont
        Director
        Les Beaux Arts Gallery
        12 Soho Boulevard
        Trendville, AZ 12345

FROM: Harold Davis
         Wilderness Studio, Inc.
         New York, NY

Enclosed please find:

Subject/Description	Format:	35mm	4X5	Contacts	Other	Value
General selection of Harold Davis color landscapes. Duplicate slides submitted per discussion for your files; holding fees waived; to be returned upon request; Thank you.		20				

Kindly check count and acknowledge by signing and returning one copy. Count shall be considered accurate and quality deemed satisfactory for reproduction if said copy is not immediately received by return mail with exceptions duly noted.

Total Black & White:
Total Color: 20

Terms of delivery:
1. After 14 days the following holding fees are charged until return: $5.00 per week per color transparency and $1.00 per week per print. 2. Submission is for examination only. Photographs may not be reproduced, copied, projected, or used in any way without (a) express written permission on our invoice stating the rights granted and the terms thereof; and (b) payment of said invoice. The reasonable and stipulated fee for any other usage shall be three (3) times our normal fee for such usage. 3. Submission is conditioned on return of all delivered items safely, undamaged, and in the condition delivered. Recipient assumes insurer's liability, not bailee's, for such return prepaid and fully insured by bonded messenger, air freight, or registered mail. Recipient assumes full liability for its employees, agents, assigns, messengers, and freelance researchers for any loss, damage or misuses of the photographs. 4. Reimbursement for loss or damage shall be determined by the value of the photographs, which recipient agrees shall be no less than a reasonable minimum of $1,500.00 for each transparency except as noted above. 5. Objection to these terms must be made in writing within five (5) days of the receipt of this Memo. Holding the material referenced herein constitutes acceptance of these terms. 6. Any dispute in connection with this Memo including its validity, interpretation, performance or breach, shall be arbitrated in New York, NY pursuant to the rules of the American Arbitration Association and the laws of the State of New York. Judgment on the arbitration award may be entered in the highest federal or state court having jurisdiction. Recipient shall pay all arbitration and court costs, reasonable attorney's fees, plus legal interest on any award or judgment. 7. Recipient agrees that the above terms are made pursuant to Article 2 of the U.C.C. and agrees to be bound by the same, including specifically the above Clause #6 to arbitrate disputes.

***ACKNOWLEDGED AND ACCEPTED: _____

ing inspection to two weeks will almost never apply. Either do not include it in your Delivery Memo, or cross it out. Otherwise expect it to be ignored. Calendar publishers plan to hold work for long periods of time due to the long lead time involved in calendar production. However, they are professionals and will do their best to return first cut rejections as speedily as possible.

It is best to submit duplicate large format (4"X5" or 8"X10") transparencies to the calendar market because there is a bias in favor of large format transparencies among calendar publishers. However, making or having large format transparencies made can be expensive, and artists may not feel that the potential returns from licensing work to calendar publishers justifies the expense of the large transparencies. For more information about transparency size and reproduction, see Chapter 3, *The Print Reproduction Process from A to Z* and Chapter 4, *Creating a Design for Publication.*

Fees for licensing work to calendar publishers are subject to negotiation like any other fees although some calendar publishers follow a fixed rate schedule for all artists published in their calendars. One example of this is the Sierra Club calendars. However, publication in the Sierra Club calendars is sufficiently prestigious for the photographers involved—exposure in the Sierra Club calendars often leads to additional stock sales and assignment work—and the fee paid can be considered only part of the compensation.

Many factors go into pricing the stock license for an image including the reproduction size, projected press run, reputation of the artist, rarity of the image, and whether the calendar is a wall-hanger (higher per-image fee because only twelve images are used) or a desk top. See the *Resources Section* for books with advice on negotiating licensing fees. A <u>range</u> of usage fees that have been paid for calendar imagery is $50.00-$2000.00 for each image. The realistic range for an average licensing fee for calendar usage is probably from $200.00 to $500.00.

Artists should be sure that the term of the license granted is spelled out in writing, e.g., Exclusive North American calendar rights to use "My Image" for a period of three years. See the section on "Financial and Legal Considerations" in Chapter 6, *How to Find Greeting Card Publishers for your Work* for further discussion of licensing.

One interesting possibility is to place your work with an agency, termed a "stock agent," who will act as your representative and handle all the details of placing work with calendar publishers and negotiating fees. This might make the most sense in getting your work sold to markets you could not otherwise reach. For example, there is a huge market in Japan for distinguished corporate calendars. The only practical way for an American artist to sell into that market is to place work with a Japanese stock agency.

But beware! Stock agents take a large

commission, often 50% of the licensing fee. They do not always reliably report sales. It is easy to give work to an agent, but it can be difficult to get it back.

Artists should be sure that any agent they deal with has a reputation for honesty. (Check with other artists the agency represents.) Do not enter into an agreement with a stock agency without learning about the agency and about the business of stock agencies. (See the *Resources Section* for books that contain more information on this topic.)

PACKAGING A CALENDAR OF YOUR OWN

An exciting possibility is to present a theme calendar of one's own to calendar publishers. Generally, to successfully package a calendar there must be a theme beyond, say, "The Watercolors of Jane Artist." With few exceptions—such as Ansel Adams, Georgia O'Keefe and Claude Monet—an artist's reputation alone is not enough to carry a calendar. But, while "The Watercolors of Jane Artist" probably will not fly, "Gardens of Southern France: The Watercolors of Jane Artist" or "Mission Era Collectibles: Drawings by Jane Artist" might.

Research is the key to finding an appropriate theme. Try to get a good feeling for calendar themes that have been pub-

lished in the past. When you pick one or two to present yourself, do not slavishly imitate something that has already been done. On the other hand, do not deviate too much from the kind of subject matter that traditionally works as a calendar theme.

Some 1994 calendar themes include "Twentieth-Century American Folk Art" from Abbeville Press, "Wooden Boats" from Addison-Wesley, "Science Fiction Art of Frank Frazetta" from Avalanche Publishing, "Arts & Crafts of Mexico" from Chronicle Books, "H.R. Giger Calendar of the Fantastique" from Morpheus International (Giger won an Oscar for his design of the alien in "Alien"), "Goddesses: The Paintings of Susan Seddon Boulet" from Pomegranate Publications, and "Gardens: An Engagement Calendar" from Stewart Tabori & Chang. The point is that there is a great variety of possible themes. But to successfully sell a calendar to a publisher (this is called "packaging") it must have an easily perceived marketable theme.

To the artist there are two big advantages to packaging a calendar to a publisher as opposed to merely licensing individual images to the publisher. First, a packaged calendar will usually prominently feature the artist's name on its cover and in its promotional material; in any case, it is a spectacular and prestigious showcase of the artist's work. Second, the packager of a complete calendar is entitled to greater compensation than the licensor of individual images. This compensation might take the form of a larger fee, or, more often, of royalties and an advance. In essence, the latter arrangement is similar to those usually made with the authors of books. Any publication contract of this sort should be reviewed with care, and professional advice should be sought.

Calendar publishers can be approached with the idea for a theme by telephone or by mail. In either case, try to arrange a personal appointment if this is possible. The general rules for making submissions and for giving your work the best chance of success are outlined in Chapter 6, *How to Find Greeting Card Publishers for your Work* and Chapter 8, *How to Find a Fine Art Poster Publisher*. Be persistent but polite. If you must submit your idea as a written proposal, keep it succinct. Include visual reference material. Remember that your proposal is a sales teaser: do not include too much material, as the aim is to get the publisher to request more (or better yet, to arrange a personal interview). Always include an SASE for the return of your material.

To successfully package a theme calendar to a publisher, the artist will have to create a comprehensive dummy ("comp") that shows what his calendar will look like. This comp will be presented by mail as a follow-up to an initial proposal, or, better yet, left with the publisher following a personal interview. See Chapter 3 through Chapter 5 for further discussion of how to make a comp, which is a simple mock-up using photographic reproductions of the art. The better and more

professional your comp is, the more likely you are to be able to sell a theme calendar. As opposed to comps of cards or posters that require the placement of only one image, comps of calendars must be presented with many images bound, the way the final calendar will be. Hanging calendars should probably have photographic prints of all twelve images in place. Desk calendars need not have all 52 images but should include a substantial number of images. Desk calendar comps should be bound using an inexpensive spiral process.

If the publisher likes the job you have done creating the comp, it is very possible that he may contract with you to do the graphic design and create mechanicals for the project. If you are offered this, by all means take it. The design fee should be a substantial addition to your other income from the project, and, if you have never done this before, you will learn how. Follow directions in Chapters 3 through 5 of this book for creating and designing a project and creating a mechanical. Be sure to discuss the issue of page imposition at an early stage with the printer, as a project that involves multiple pages must be laid out in certain ways.

A theme calendar of the work of an artist presents a tremendous financial opportunity for that artist and is a wonderful way for him to showcase his work. Artists with appropriate work and the imagination to conceptualize marketable themes should not hesitate to attempt to package their own calendars.

SELF-PUBLISHING CALENDARS

In general, artists should not undertake self-publication of calendars. The only exception to this is when a distributor or buyer has contracted in advance to buy enough calendars for the artist to make a profit. An example of this might be a "private" calendar, where a company contracts to buy the entire press run of a calendar that the artist designs specifically for the company which intends to use it for promotional purposes. In this situation, essentially the artist has packaged his calendar to the company with his fee being the difference between the contract price and production costs.

Another example would be if a distributor or chain of retail stores agreed in advance to purchase enough copies of the calendar to make it worthwhile.

Calendars are difficult to self-publish profitably because:

(1) They must be produced far in advance of the year of their use;

(2) They are a dated item with only a short temporal window of sales opportunity;

(3) It is difficult to get distribution for self-publishing without a broad line of different calendars;

(4) Press runs of 10,000 copies or more are required to bring the per unit cost down to a place where the calendar can profitably be marketed;

(5) A single error in the calendar (as opposed to the artwork) portion of the project, such as the wrong day of the week with a given date, can make the entire project unmarketable.

While for the reasons enumerated above artists should avoid self-publishing calendars in most circumstances, if most or all of the press run can be pre-sold, it may make financial sense to do so. Artists should also be aware, as noted in the previous section, that packaging their ideas for theme calendars to publishers is potentially very feasible, lucrative and prestigious. Furthermore, it avoids the financial risks and business drudgery of self-publishing calendars.

It is the narrow period during which calendars can be sold, unlike cards, books or posters which in theory can be sold forever, that hammers the nail in the coffin of self-publication of calendars. It is almost impossible to make money on a first calendar publication venture because profitability requires a distribution network to be in place at the time of publication. Successful self-publication of calendars thus becomes, at best, a multi-year process, with financial rewards deferred and building a publishing business essential. However, artists should take heart: there are myriad opportunities for licensing imagery to the calendar industry, and calendar publishers are always open to professional quality packages that are presented to them. ◆

11.

A More Detailed Look at the Self-Publishing Option

This chapter examines several important topics. First, starting a self-publishing business is not for everybody. How can you decide if it is for you? The chapter continues with a discussion of general business issues—common to any kind of business, not just self-publishing—that fledgling entrepreneurs must cope with. It concludes with some suggestions about how artists who self-publish can integrate their artistic side with their business role.

IS SELF-PUBLISHING FOR YOU?

To self-publish involves starting a self-publishing business. Starting a self-publishing business—starting any business—should not be undertaken lightly.

A business—particularly a young one—is like a child: to grow and prosper it needs plenty of attention and love. Some day the business—like a grown child taking care of his aged parents—may support you. However, initially the proposition is reversed. Your time and money go into getting the business started. There is often very little initial return. Eventually, this situation can be reversed. A self-publishing business can become a tremendously enabling vehicle for the creative artist by providing financial support for the artist and a method for the dissemination of his work. Before that situation is reached there can be years of struggle. Potential self-publishers should ask themselves if they are really prepared for the financial and emotional investment that this requires.

Prior to starting a self-publication venture, the artist should take time out to become clear about his goals. Clarity, or lack of it, about his goals has a direct relationship to the success he achieves. Many self-publication ventures have mixed intentions. The goals of the project may be one part artistic, one part promotional, and one part financial. To the extent that you become clear about what is most important, you will be better at decision making. When conducting this evaluation, try to be realistic about the expected consequences of the decisions you make. For example, if you are starting a greeting card publication venture, are you truly willing to take the time to create a network of sales representatives? *Publishing Your Art As Cards, Posters & Calendars* provides information in sufficient detail so that even the novice self-publisher—if he is prepared to see the world with open eyes and to conduct research as the book suggests—can predict the likely consequences of his actions.

The self-publisher should be prepared to <u>plan</u> in as great detail as possible. No doubt the plan will be deviated from down the road. For the time being, plan exactly what you want to produce, what it will cost, where the money will come from to finance it, and how it will be produced, sold, distributed and fulfilled. Put your plan in writing. Show it to friends (particularly those who are knowledgeable about business, marketing, art or publishing) whom you feel will give you objective advice. Listen to them. Do not necessarily be dissuaded from your project by their comments. Use their ideas to make your publication venture more likely to succeed.

A potential self-publisher has an initial advantage if he has some business background (either academic or practical). At the least, the self-publisher should realize that starting a business will require spending much time attending to business matters. If the self-publisher has no prior experience with business, he must be prepared to become educated and to work hard at being a business person as well as an artist.

People do things well if they enjoy doing them. Take an honest inventory of what you like doing. Often—although not always—artists do not like performing business tasks. In this case, they probably will not do them well. While it is appropriate to undertake a certain amount of activity that is a chore rather than a joy, too many chores are a sure prescription for disaster.

Consider carefully your aversion to risk. If taking chances makes you uncomfortable, do not start a business, and do not consider self-publishing. By its very nature, a self-publishing venture involves risk. The returns may be great, but the risk cannot be avoided. If worrying about the risk is going to drive you crazy and lead to sleepless nights, don't take the plunge. It isn't worth it.

Do you have the money to finance a self-publishing venture? If not, how do you plan to finance it? Without a realistic financing plan—discussed in the next section—a self-publishing venture should not be considered.

How will self-publishing fit in with your artistic goals? A related question is, how important is total control over your work to you? One great benefit of self-publishing is that—within the limits of your financing—you have complete control of the design and final appearance of your work. On the other hand, some artists prefer to have professional publishers who understand marketing and distribution shape the design of their reproduced work. If you don't have some ability with design and a feel for what works in the marketplace, it is probably true that you will do better to let a publisher—and the publisher's design staff—make the crucial decisions.

As this discussion suggests, the decision to self-publish involves making trade-offs. Potential self-publishers must be honest with themselves about their strengths, weaknesses, resources and what they like doing to make this decision with as much clarity as possible.

STARTING A BUSINESS

Starting a business requires a plan. As the previous section indicates, before you make the decision to start a self-publishing business, it is a good idea to plan as much as possible and to put your ideas on paper so you can discuss them clearly with advisers. Once you have definitely decided to start the business, a written financial plan becomes mandatory. This kind of plan involves a much greater level of detail than merely writing down your ideas about a potential new business. Largely its format has become formalized.

There are several books—and even computer software—that can help you write a business plan (see *Resources Section*). Often, a business plan is a rather stylized document that is primarily intended to help obtain financing. An equally important, if not more important, role of the formal business plan is as a problem solving tool. It is much better to spot potential pitfalls early rather than later when it may be too late to do anything about them. In addition, a business plan is a standardized kind of document that financial experts can evaluate and give advice about.

As a minimum, a business plan should include detailed and specific information on the following questions:

(1) What is the product to be made? What will it cost? What will it be sold for? How will it be marketed and distributed? What is the competition?

(2) Who will do what in running the business? Why are they competent to do so?

(3) How much will it cost to start the business? How much more money will it require in its first three years? What interest or equity participation in the business must be given in exchange for the financing?

(4) Will the business pay you a salary? If not, what will you live on?

(5) Precisely how will the costs of capitalizing the business be repaid? When will

this money be repaid?

In addition, the plan should provide estimated financial statements for the first three years of operation based on reasonable and justifiable assumptions about sales and the costs of doing business. Your assumptions, and their justifications, should be explained. Finally, if you personally will be financing a major portion of the venture, a personal financial statement should be included.

I know this sounds like a lot of work, and it is. But starting and running a business involves a great deal more. It makes sense to do your homework in advance to give your venture the best chance of success. (If you cannot bring yourself to prepare a formal business plan, then you should not be starting a business at all!) Preparation of a solid plan confers the following benefits:

(1)   You will have already thought about many of the major difficulties that may arise, and will have solutions to some of them.

(2)   Your financial projections should make it less likely that you are undercapitalized, one of the biggest causes of failure in start-up ventures.

(3)   Your business plan is a document that can be reviewed and discussed by financial and business experts. If you have a plan, you are more likely to get good advice.

(4)   A solid plan is an essential requirement for obtaining third-party financial backing.

Self-publishers should make a decision about what kind of entity they wish their new business to be. There are three possibilities: a sole proprietorship, a partnership, and a corporation (see below for a brief discussion of the consequences of each selection). Before making this decision, it is essential to get legal advice and input from a competent accountant on the potential taxation consequences. In general, it is extremely important to make sure all record keeping and filing requirements of federal, state and local governments are met. This may require setting up your calendar to remind you when specific forms are due.

As a minimum, you will be required to get a Federal Employer Identification Number ("EIN") for your business. Get your accountant or lawyer to help you with this, or contact the Internal Revenue Service directly and request Form SS-4, "Application for Employer Identification Number." This form is simple and straightforward to complete, and the IRS is generally quite helpful with it. The EIN is to a business what the social security number is to an individual. Taxes and other governmental filings are identified using the EIN. Money that is paid to your business that for one reason or another must be reported to the government is reported on a Form 1099 using the EIN (if the money had been paid to you individually, your social security number would have been used).

In most jurisdictions, businesses are required to collect state and local sales taxes. (Some states use the EIN, but others assign their own identification numbers to businesses.) Money collected must later be turned over to the state. Even if you do not collect any sales tax (perhaps because all of your sales are wholesale), you will still be required to make regular sales tax filings (either quarterly or annually). If you neglect to do so, even if you owe no money, you will be fined.

Your business will also be responsible for withholding income and social security taxes for your employees and for payroll taxes.

A sole proprietorship is the simplest business organization. As the name suggests, it is a business run by a single person. Federal income taxes on a sole proprietorship are calculated on Form 1040, Schedule C, "Profit or Loss From Business (Sole Proprietorship)." Sole proprietors are generally required to file a fictitious business certificate at their local county clerk's office. This filing is also known as a "DBA" or "Doing Business As." There is usually a nominal cost for filing a DBA.

Sole proprietors should exercise great care not to mingle business and personal funds. From this point of view, the business must have its own checking account. Most banks will require a copy of the DBA to open an account in the business name.

Partnerships, whose income is reported to the federal government using Form 1065, can be a good choice of business organization when two or more people are involved. Great care must be taken, however, to have a well thought out written partnership agreement drafted by a knowledgeable lawyer.

Starting your own corporation is not a very difficult process. In most states, it costs between $150.00 and $700.00 to start a corporation, including filing fees, a name search and legal advice. Beyond these initial costs, your corporation will be subject to a Federal Corporation Income Tax, meaning that your income may be taxed twice, once when it is paid to the corporation and once when it is paid by your corporation to you as salary or dividends. Also, corporations are subject to various state and local taxes. Often these taxes have surprisingly hefty minimums (due even if your corporation makes no money).

There are also, it should come as no surprise to those who dwell in contemporary America, many advantages to the corporation as a business entity. Chief among these is legal insulation of the owners of the business for claims against the corporation. Also significant is the income tax deductibility of certain items not deductible by sole proprietorships. For example, currently a corporation can deduct health insurance premiums paid for its employees as a business expense. A sole proprietor cannot.

Obviously, if you are considering forming a corporation, you need expert advice about the pros and cons.

Whichever form of business entity you select, it will do you no good unless you can capitalize your venture. There are no magic formulas for raising money. A good first step is to be realistic about how much you need. It is probably more than you think at first. Your business plan should help clarify this.

Of course, the easiest thing is if you have the money yourself and are willing to risk losing it. If you do not, family, friends and financial institutions will have to be approached. It is essential to have a business plan at this stage.

Beware of borrowing from family and friends. By definition, a new venture involves some risk. There is always the possibility that the venture will not succeed and that the investment will be lost. This is a great way to lose friends. In any case, investments or loans from friends or family members should be treated as a business matter. Terms, interest and a repayment schedule should be agreed upon. The agreement should be in writing and signed by both parties.

If your financial plan is businesslike and reasonable, there is a good chance of obtaining financing from a bank. Banks will require that you personally guarantee their loan (whether or not your business is a corporation). Also, your chances will be better if you have a prior relationship with the bank and are yourself providing equity financing.

Before making any substantial loan, a responsible bank will want to know that there are two ways in which it can recover its money. First, cash flow from the business should be sufficient to cover interest payments and amortize the principal. Second, there should be a source of repayment in case of business failure. This is not what the person starting a small business wants to hear, but it is the truth. The smaller the loan requested, the more stringent the bank will be. For example, it is quite possible that a self-publishing artist might have to take out a second mortgage on his home to get financing. (But wait, you ask: What about Donald Trump? The S&L Bandits? Another story completely. Those rogues are big time.) Someone starting a business has to expect to place his equity at risk in order to get financing. If you can't stand the heat, get out of the kitchen.

One final—and under exploited—source of financing is suppliers. Suppliers such as printers have a strong interest in the success of publishing businesses. They may be willing to extend very favorable payment terms. If so, this should be negotiated clearly in advance. Trust is a required element. "Ooops, I can't pay you this month," is not the right approach and will not lead to long term support from vendors.

RUNNING A BUSINESS

Your business is a projection of yourself, your goals and your ideals. As much care should be given to planning how it will be run as would be given to creating a major work of art. Businesses that work do so in large part because of clean and clear communication among owners, employees, customers and suppliers. Customers and potential customers sense clarity of communication and respond to it. They know they will generally get what they have been told they will get. If there is a problem, it will be acknowledged in a straightforward, responsible way.

The single most important component of clear business communication is telling the truth. This is often not as easy as it sounds. Be honest about what you promise you can do. Do not overly exaggerate the benefits of your products.

While there is never an excuse for lack of courtesy, customers, employees and suppliers must be told in a straightforward way when they are wrong. You will also have to acknowledge as soon as it becomes apparent when you have made a mistake.

Businesses that are run along these lines, and where effort and thought go into the preparation of promotional materials as well as the product, tend to thrive.

One of the tougher chores faced by the small business is collecting unpaid accounts. These funds can be vital to the survival of the business. The small business owner fears that pushing too hard can alienate customers, but he needs the money.

There are some unpleasant facts about collections that must be kept in mind:

(1) There is no practical way to force the payment of small debts, unless the debtor wishes to continue to do business with you (in which case he will pay so that you will ship him more product).

(2) Some of your customers will, to the extent you let them, put off paying you and capture the "float" (accrued interest) on the money that has remained in their account instead of paying you on time.

(3) As a statistical matter, the longer a payment is past due, the less likely it is that it will ever be paid in full.

The consequence of these statements, particularly the final one, is that collection activity must start early. By the time a bill has become badly past due, it is far too late. Collection activity should be a planned affair that should begin before a bill is due at all.

"Net 30 Days," meaning that an invoice should be paid within thirty days, constitutes normal commercial payment terms. On a Net 30 Days invoice, two statements should go out before the thirty-day period is up. If the bill hasn't been paid within thirty days, another reminder should go out. At thirty days plus a few extra days for the check to arrive in the mail, the customer should be contacted to find out if there is a problem.

Customer contacts regarding collections

should be carefully scripted in advance. Don't be a wimp! On the other hand, don't be rude. First contacts should have as their goal establishing a payment date and nothing more. "When can I expect the check?" is the correct question. If you are told, "The check is in the mail," or a variant, get a check number and date. Make sure to get the name of the person you talked to, and note it in your file. If necessary, move politely but firmly up the ladder of authority at the company until you reach someone who will promise you a payment date. Then, follow up on the promise if the check doesn't arrive. The correct tone is firm, polite, and, no matter what happens, more of sorrow than anger. Remember that adherence to the social contract on the part of your debtor and his desire for more of your goods are essentially the only reasons he has for paying you. An overtly hostile tone may rend the fabric of the social contract beyond mending. You may also lose the client for good. (Sometimes this is to be desired, of course. New merchandise should almost never be shipped to customers with outstanding past due balances.) Collection must simply be regarded as a natural part of the business process, not one that should generate a tremendous amount of emotion on your part.

When the shoe is on the other foot—meaning you are writing checks, not invoices—the golden rule applies. Do as you would be done to. If possible, pay your bills on time. It is almost always a business mistake to try to capture the float by holding onto money that does not belong

to you. Whatever small sum you make in interest is more than offset by the ill will created in your suppliers, who do notice late payments. Don't you?

If for any reason you must delay payments, then do so in a planned and responsible way. Talk to your suppliers. As long as vendors are provided in advance with a payment schedule, they are likely to go along with it.

One of the most difficult challenges for the small business owner is the hiring and retention of good employees. Self-publishers in particular tend to dream of hiring efficient office managers and going back to being primarily artists. But it is not so easy to do so. Good people you can trust are hard to find. Will you really be able to offer them competitive salaries, benefits and security? And no one else is as motivated as you are. It is your business, after all.

There is no easy rule of thumb that will help self-publishers hire and keep good employees. But these tips will help:

(1) When writing the job description (or help wanted ad), emphasize the unique aspects of the opportunity you are offering. For example, is it a ground floor opportunity to get in on a business that will become much bigger? Is there an opportunity for expression of personal creativity? Is it a chance to learn new skills? Are hours flexible?

(2) Besides writing a detailed job descrip-

tion, prepare a questionnaire that every applicant should complete.

(3) Be sure to obtain references, both personal and professional. Check them before hiring anyone. When discussing an applicant with someone given as a reference, be sure to listen for what is not said as much as what is said.

(4) Be aware that discrimination is illegal.

(5) Hire people you like and feel you can get along with. Hopefully, you will be working with them for a long time.

(6) Do not ask employees to do anything you have not done at least once yourself.

(7) Do not expect anybody to be as motivated as you are. It is your business.

(8) Prepare an office manual (see below) that details the way things should be done in your business.

(9) Provide periodic formal performance reviews for each employee. Good performance should be rewarded, both materially and verbally.

(10) Move quickly to resolve any situations in which an employee is not working out. Find a solution that satisfies you and the employee, or fire him.

(11) Delegate responsibility responsibly by providing guidelines sufficient to get a chore done without always leaning over your employee's shoulders.

An office manual should be prepared. (Computer software is available with model manuals which can be adapted to your specific needs.) The primary purpose of the office manual is to clarify all procedures that the business initiates or handles. How does an order get processed? How are bills paid? How are employee hours recorded? The office manual is valuable for training new staff. It also helps ensure the continuity of the business when a key employee such as an office manager quits. Finally, the act of preparing the manual involves careful analysis of exactly how things are done. It is likely that some improvements will become apparent. Your office manual should be placed in a looseleaf binder and updated periodically.

No business today can afford not to be computerized. The advent of inexpensive and powerful "personal" computers and laser printers have enabled small businesses to deliver a business work product—financial paperwork, business documents and correspondence—comparable in quality to that of the largest corporations. In addition, computers can handle many of the more repetitive chores of accounting, inventory control and database management, thus freeing humans for more creative endeavors.

This wonderful and powerful tool, the computer, does, however, exact a price. Its effective use requires considerable expertise. The small business owner has no choice but to become as educated as possible about computers. In addition, the business may need to contract with expert computer consultants for help. (Word of mouth from other small business owners is the best way to find a consultant who is competent and likely to understand your needs.) Making sure that any potential employee is computer literate before hiring him is also an extremely good idea.

The material in this section covers much ground. In fact, it has touched only the surface of the issues that rise in running a business. To succeed with a self-publishing venture, education about business issues must be regarded as ongoing and continuous. Difficulties must be met with imagination, courage, resilience and the willingness to improvise. A business that is run in this spirit has a great chance of success.

INTEGRATION OF ARTISTIC AND BUSINESS PURSUITS

In our society, most artists have a very difficult role. It may take many years—if it ever happens—for even the most talented and productive artist to be able to support himself with his work. Meanwhile, the artist has to make a living while staying creative. This amounts to two jobs, which often do not overlap. In the context of this discussion, the first job is being an artist. The second is founding and running a self-publishing business.

There is no magical formula for staying creative as an artist while self-publishing. But these are some suggestions that others have found helpful.

(1) Put aside quality time solely for artistic creation. Particularly if your artistic work is going slowly, this may seem difficult to justify from a business point of view. However, it is essential. Without adequate time to create, you will no longer be an artist.

(2) Separate your need for praise of your work from your need for sales in your business. As an artist you should strive to be the best you can be and to satisfy only yourself. As a business person, you should learn to treat financial matters objectively. In either case, sales in dollars—or lack of them—do not truly reflect on the merit of the work sold.

(3) Enjoy what you do. Take pride and pleasure in your work both as business person and artist.

(4) Do not tolerate boredom. If you become bored, try changing your routine or accepting new challenges.

(5) Do not stand still in your work. Strive to constantly grow. Accept that not everyone will like your latest work. Creativity—and the interests of a true artist—goes in cycles. At different times you will be into doing different things. This is as it should be.

(6) Do not neglect your personal relationships, physical health and spiritual

well being.

The ideal self-publishing business is one that supports and complements an artistic career, not one that distracts from it and competes with it. If you put the same creative energies into your self-publishing business that you do into your artwork, and continue to grow as an artist, you are quite likely to prosper in both realms. With clarity of vision, careful planning, and a thorough study of the relevant chapters of this book, the resulting business is likely to approach the ideal. In this case, you will benefit personally and financially. In addition, your artwork will grow bolder, will become more experimental and will thrive. ◆

12.

Commonly Asked Questions and Answers

Over the years since the first edition of *Publishing Your Art As Cards & Posters* appeared, I have received many letters with questions related to the publication of art and self-publishing. While these letters tended to reflect the personal situations and concerns of their authors, many questions seemed of general interest and were raised repeatedly. I am reproducing below concise answers to the most commonly asked questions.

■ *I would like to get my work published. What is the best way to get started?*

It is best to first attempt to get your art published by a reputable card, poster or calendar publisher. If your work is accepted, it is a credential that will lead to further publication. Try to find a publisher whose products are similar but not identical with your artwork. Detailed discussions of researching and approaching publishers will be found in Chapter 6,

How to Find Greeting Card Publishers for your Work, Chapter 8, *How to Find a Fine Art Poster Publisher*, and Chapter 10, *The Calendar Market*.

■ *I am considering trying to get some of my work published. How do I submit work?*

Please review the sections on "Making a Submission" in Chapter 6, *How to Find Greeting Card Publishers for your Work* and "How to Submit Work to an Art Poster Publisher" in Chapter 8. In general, first contact the publisher, and find out in what form they would like to see work. Slides are usually best. Do not send too many. Label them neatly with your name. Be sure to enclose an SASE.

■ *Why is publication important for the artist?*

In addition to providing a source of income, publication of an artist's work as cards, posters and calendars is a prestigious and career-enhancing event that in all likelihood will lead to many different kinds of opportunities.

■ *What kinds of imagery is marketable as cards? As posters? As calendars?*

It is hard to make across the board generalizations, and many different kinds of imagery sell to publishers and consumers in these different markets. To succeed in these fields, work must be high quality and professional. But taking a stab at generalizing, card imagery is humorous or nostalgic and related to card-sending occasions, such as birthdays. Poster art that succeeds often relates to current interior design trends. Imagery is of the quality that people are prepared to live with for a long time. Calendar art is salable when it presents a top quality evocation of collectible objects or places of special interest to a specific group of people.

■ *I have been approached by a fine art poster publisher who would like me to design a poster using my watercolors that he will publish. The publisher has asked me to quote a flat fee for the design work and for the use of my art. How do I determine a fair fee?*

It is always strategically wise to let the purchaser quote first. Ask the publisher what his budget is. Review the material in the "Contractual Terms and Economic Considerations" section of Chapter 8, *How to*

Find a Fine Art Publisher. Get qualified advice before signing the contract.

■ *Why haven't more well-known artists decided to self-publish?*

In fact, many have. But the decision to self-publish is a personal one. Some well-known artists don't want to take the time out from their artistic work that starting and running a self-publishing venture requires. They may also not be educated about the potential profitability in self-publishing.

■ *Do major poster publishers license imagery from stock agencies? If so, wouldn't the best approach for an artist be to find a good agent?*

The decision of whether to work with a stock agent is, once again, a personal one. The chief advantage of stock agencies is that your work is marketed and licensed without effort on your part. Drawbacks include loss of control over the uses of your work and the sales commissions paid to the agent.

Stock agencies are far more involved with photography than they are with other forms of art. Calendar and card publishers <u>do</u> obtain a significant portion of their imagery via stock agencies. Fine art poster publishers are less likely to do so, not because they have anything against working with agencies but rather because the kind of unique qualities that makes for a successful poster is not very often found at an agency.

■ *I am enclosing a copy of a Christmas card I published last year. The image on the card is of the seasonal lighting at a nearby tourist attraction. To my surprise, it sold very well. Now I would like to make a poster from the image. What advice do you have?*

Try to keep production costs down on the poster so that it can be successfully sold as a retail tourist and gift item. The retail price should be less than $10.00. (Of course, you must be able to make money at this price.) Design a point-of-purchase display and gift containers for the poster so merchants in the area of the tourist attraction can easily sell your poster.

■ *I have been selling a poster of My City's skyline. It has done fairly well locally. My copies of the poster were provided to me free of charge in exchange for a license to my client to use my image on his trade show poster. I would like to market this poster to stores nationally. My plan would be to sell directly, bypassing distributors and keeping more of the profit. What is the best way to do this? I have considered advertising in "Decor" and getting a booth at trade shows.*

Color advertisements in *Decor* or *Art Business News* are quite expensive. (There is no point in advertising a color work of art in black and white.) The major publishers who use this approach do not expect to make their money back in imme-

diate sales. Their advertising campaigns are long-term. It is not likely that there will be many sales with only one or two ads. Your limited product selection is also a problem. Similarly, I would not expect to make my money back through direct sales from exhibiting at a trade show. My advice is to invest your money in creating additional posters instead of in advertising. Once you have found some national distributors for your line, you can also attempt to market it directly if you wish. If you attempt to do this, you must create a pricing structure that allows for the possibility (see Chapter 9, *Self-Publishing and Distributing Art Posters*).

■ *How can I learn about digital imaging and the new computer technologies as they apply to photography and other art?*

Take courses at institutions that specialize in these fields such as New York's School of Visual Arts or Camden, Maine's Center for Creative Imaging. Get a computer, if you don't already have one, and learn to use illustration programs and image manipulation programs such as Photo-Shop and PhotoStyler.

■ *Your book does not include information on marketing limited edition prints. How can I find distributors and publishers of limited edition prints?*

The market for limited edition prints is entirely different from the market for cards, posters and calendars. Both *Decor* and *Art Business News* (see *Resources Section*) do publish annual Sources Directories. While these are compiled from the point of view of galleries and frame shops who wish to purchase art and related products, they do contain listings for every major distributor of limited edition graphics in the country and are the best source for this information. A number of other books listed in the Bibliography offer additional information.

■ *How can I find out about grants to artists? Might I be able to use a grant to help start a self-publishing business?*

The best source for information about grants and foundations is:

The Foundation Center
79 Fifth Avenue
New York, NY 10003
800-424-9836; 212-620-4230.

Only a few grants are made directly to individual artists. Most of these are quite well-known (for example, the National Endowment Visual Artist program). The fact is that, by law, most foundations are not allowed to give money to individuals. They are required to give their money to registered charitable institutions. In addition, most foundations will not knowingly fund a profit-making venture. So, on the whole, this would not seem to be a good source of financing for a self-publishing business.

■ *How can I find sales representatives to sell my cards?*

Ask card store owners for the names of sales reps they like dealing with. Network at trade shows such as the National Stationery Show. Ask sales reps you do find for names of sales reps in other parts of the country.

■ *I would like to make a business out of selling my handmade cards. Is this a practical idea?*

It depends on how many cards you want to make and how much your time is worth. Since most cards sell for under $2.00, meaning the publisher's share is substantially less than $1.00, you will have to manually create many cards very quickly to make any money. ◆

13.

Conclusion

Publishing Your Art As Cards, Posters & Calendars is intended to be used by you as a tool to enable you to achieve your dreams. This book does not pull punches. It tells it like it is. It includes a great wealth of technical information and discusses in depth the practical realities of business. If you have work that is appropriate, if you read this book carefully, and if you follow its suggestions, then you <u>will</u> be published.

The first step down this road is to believe in yourself as a human being and as an artist. Learn to make decisions based on what feels right. Listen to your inner voice when you make your decisions. Suggestions are often good—pay attention to them; take them seriously. But don't be so swayed by them that your art turns into something it isn't. Next thing you know, your giraffe is merely a horse with spots. Trust yourself to know what is right for you. You alone are responsible for creating your art. You alone are responsible for seeing that it gets published. Some-

times the decisions that you must make based on this responsibility require taking a leap of faith when all the world seems to be against your ideas. By all means take the leap, but only after you have thoroughly researched reproduction processes, graphic design, marketing, financing and distribution—in short, the topics covered in this book.

An artist's career must stand or fall based on a body of work. A single image is not remotely enough. Your first publication should not be your last. This means that you must keep moving, in your work and in your publication projects. Always think ahead, plan ahead, and work ahead. If you find yourself in a time of lack of inspiration, look deep inside yourself and find one thing, one idea. It doesn't matter much what it is. Think of the one little idea as a flower. Meditate on the idea. Follow its flow as though it were a river. Soon your one little flower has turned into a big, beautiful flowering bush. Try to look at the world with a different point of view every day for a few moments. Use your altered consciousness about the unchanged world around you to claim for yourself new inspiration and new ideas.

Treat yourself well. Your good health is just as important to your ability to create or publish art as the art is. Nurture yourself. Be kind to yourself. Let yourself have room to grow. Give yourself permission to do what you want to do. Try not to be such a perfectionist that you stifle yourself. Allow yourself room to experiment and make mistakes. Some of your publication ventures may not succeed. This is normal. If they all did succeed it would mean you are not taking enough chances. It's okay to say, "I may not be perfect now. I will allow myself the space and time to grow into what I want to be. I will move on to the next project."

Internalize the thought that you can have the career that you want to have. Be open to prosperity, creativity and inspiration. Allow them to come to you. Do not limit yourself. Be a practical romantic. Every artist owes it to himself to be pragmatic and responsible in his relationship with the world of business and money.

Have fun! Please have fun! Don't turn into a pompous angst-ridden artist. The temperamental artist is a stupid, unnecessary cliché. Life is too short not to enjoy it. Use publication and self-publication of your art to further you along your path and as a vehicle that serves you. Use it to increase your joy.

Don't postpone doing what you want to do. You've made a good start by buying this book. Now, take another step. Create a plan of action based on what you have read. Make a commitment to getting your work published. Take some concrete action towards that goal every single day. If not now, when?

I sincerely hope that *Publishing Your Art As Cards, Posters & Calendars* has been informative and has proved helpful to you. I would welcome hearing about your progress in this field. Please write to me in care of the publisher. ◆

Appendix I

BIBLIOGRAPHY

Adobe Type Guide. Two Volumes. Mountain View, Ca: Adobe Systems Inc., 1991. [800-833-6687. The most complete catalog of fonts (typefaces) suitable for quality reproduction and generally available to designers, service bureaus, printers and publishers.]

ASMP. *Stock Photography Handbook.* 2nd ed. New York: American Society of Media Photographers, 1990. [How to sell photography as stock. Much of the material on negotiating imagery licenses applies to other media as well as photography. Note that the First Edition of this book contains a pricing guide with actual dollar numbers (the Second Edition does not).]

Beach, Mark, Steve Shepro, and Ken Russon. *Getting It Printed: How to Work with Printers and Graphic Arts Services to Assure Quality, Stay on Schedule, and Control Costs.* Portland, Or.: Coast to Coast Books, 1986. [An excellent manual on the printing process and how to work with printers. See particularly the discussion of papers.]

Biedny, David and Bert Monroy. *The Official Adobe PhotoShop Handbook.* New York: Bantam Books, 1991. [How to use PhotoShop, a leading image manipulation computer program.]

Crawford, Tad. *Legal Guide for the Visual Artist.* Rev. ed. New York: Madison Square Press, 1990.

Davis, Harold. *Photographer's Publishing Handbook.* New York: Images Press, 1991. [How to get a photography book published.]

_____. *Successful Fine Art Photography.* New York: Images Press, 1992. [How to make a living as a fine art photographer.]

Engh, Rohn. *Sell & Re-Sell Your Photos.* 2nd edition. Cincinnati: Writer's Digest Books, 1992. [One of the best guides to selling stock photography.]

Franklin-Smith, Constance. *Art Marketing Handbook for the Fine Artist.* Renaissance, Ca.: ArtNetwork Press, 1992.

_____. *Art Marketing Sourcebook for the Fine Artist.* Renaissance, Ca.: ArtNetwork Press, 1992.

Graphic Artists Guild. *Graphic Artists Guild Handbook Pricing & Ethical Guidelines.* Seventh Edition. New York: Graphic Artists Guild, 1991.

Hart, Russell. *Photographing Your Artwork.* Cincinnati: North Light Books, 1987. [How to make slides from your artwork.]

Hoover, Deborah A. *Supporting Youself as an Artist.* 2nd ed. New York: Oxford University Press, 1989. [This book contains good information for those seeking support from sources other than the sale of their work, e.g., foundations, patrons and residencies.]

Klayman, Toby Judith and Cobbett Steinberg. *The Artist's Survival Manual: A Complete Guide to Marketing your Work.* New York: Charles Scribner, 1984.

Kremer, John. *Directory of Book, Catalog, and Magazine Printers.* 4th ed. Fairfield, Ia.: Ad-Lib Publications, 1988. [800-624-5893. An excellent listing of printers by various criteria.]

Lem, Dean Phillip. *Graphics Master 5.* Los Angeles: Dean Lem Associates, 1991. [800-562-2562. An excellent practical reference work and resource for designers].

Marshall, Sam A., ed. *1993 Photographer's Market.* Cincinnati: Writer's Digest Books, 1993. [This directory, published annually, lists markets for photography.]

Michels, Caroll. *How to Survive & Prosper as an Artist.* New York: Henry Holt & Co., 1983.

Miller, Lauri, ed. *1993 Artist's Market.* Cincinnati: Writer's Digest Books, 1993. [This directory, published annually, lists markets for artwork.]

Persky, Robert S., ed. *Directory of Poster/Card/Calendar Publishers & Record Companies.* New York: The Consultant Press, Ltd., 1994.

_____. *Stock Photo Deskbook.* New York: The Consultant Press, Ltd., 1992. [The most complete directory of stock houses, individual, and institutional sources of stock imagery.]

Pocket Pal: A Graphic Arts Production Handbook. New York: International Paper Company, undated. [Classic paperback guide to the history, theory and practice of production and printing.]

Sinetar, Marsha. *Do What you Love, the Money Will Follow.* New York: Bantam Doubleday Dell, 1987. [How to overcome the things that stop us from doing what we really want.]

RESOURCES

Periodicals

Art Business News is a leading trade publication in tabloid format aimed at professionals in the art and framing businesses. It is published by Myers Publishing Co., Inc., 19 Old Kings Highway South, Darien, CT 06820, 203-656-3402.

Decor, "The Business Magazine of Fine Art and Framing," is somewhat glossier than *Art Business News* but aimed at the same audience. *Decor* is published by Commerce Publishing Co., 330 North Fourth Street, St. Louis, MO 63102, 314-421-5445.

Greetings Magazine, 309 Fifth Avenue, New York, NY 10016, 212-679-6677, is a trade publication that contains business news about the greeting card industry.

Printing News, 245 West 17th Street, New York, NY 10011, 212-463-6727, is a weekly trade publication aimed at the printing industry. It contains a wealth of information about trade printers and related suppliers.

Publish is a leading magazine intended to be helpful to designers and publishers using computers. Contact: International Data Group, 501 Second Street, San Francisco, CA 94107, 415-978-3820.

Publisher's Weekly, 249 West 17th Street, New York, NY 10011, 800-842-1669, is the bible of the book publishing industry. Information on the bookstore market for cards, posters and calendars is also covered.

Trade Shows

The American Booksellers Association (ABA) Convention & Trade Exhibit takes places annually in late May or early June. Location varies. The show includes a section for bookstore sideline products such as cards, posters and calendars. Contact:

American Booksellers Association
137 West 25th Street
New York, NY 10001
212-463-8450; 800-637-0037.

Art Buyers Caravan holds regional art trade shows annually in Atlanta, Dallas, Long Beach (Ca.), Louisville, Orlando and Philadelphia. For further information contact:

Director of Trade Shows
Decor Magazine
330 North Fourth Street
St. Louis, MO 63102
314-421-5445.

Artexpo in New York is the leading trade show for fine art posters. It takes place at the Javits Convention Center in New York in the spring. There is also an Artexpo held in Southern California. Contact:

Artexpo
747 Third Avenue
New York, NY 10017
212-418-4288.

The National Stationery Show is the leading trade show in the paper products industry. It is held in New Yok in the late spring. Contact:

George Little Management
2 Park Avenue
New York, NY 10016
212-686-6070.

Miscellaneous

American Council for the Arts
1285 Avenue of the Americas, 3rd floor
New York, NY 10019
212-245-4510.

ACA serves as a source of information on arts-related topics. A library and database are maintained. In cooperation with the Marie Walsh Sharpe Art Foundation, it operates the Visual Artist Information Hotline. The hotline is a referral service designed to give artists information on matters of funding, insurance, health, and law. It operates Monday through Friday, 2-5PM eastern standard time. 800-232-2789.

College Art Association
275 Seventh Avenue
New York, NY 10001
212-691-1051.

The CAA provides information on college-level teaching jobs available to artists.

Graphic Artists Guild
11 West 20th Street
New York, NY 10011
212-463-7730.

The guild represents the interests of designers, illustrators, graphic artists, computer artists and textile designers.

Jeanouard Ltd.
70 Forest Avenue, Suite D
Glen Cove, NY 11542
516-759-3040

This company is a contract fulfillment warehouse specializing in art and the fine art poster industry. While there are many general fulfillment services, Jeanouard is the only one I know of that specializes in this area.

Light Impressions
439 Monroe Avenue
Rochester, NY 14607
800-828-6216

This company produces an excellent line of products for displaying art.

PaperDirect, Inc.
205 Chubb Avenue
Lyndhurst, NJ 07071
800-A-PAPERS

An excellent source for specialty papers designed to work with laser printers.

The Pollack-Krasner Foundation
725 Park Avenue
New York, NY 10021
212-517-5400

The Pollack-Krasner Foundation makes monetary grants to "visual artists around the world who demonstrate merit and financial need." ◆

Appendix II

SELECTED IMPORTANT CARD PUBLISHERS

American Greetings
10500 American Road
Cleveland, OH 44144
216-252-7300

Hallmark Cards, Inc.
2501 McGee Street
Kansas City, MO 64108
816-274-5111

Recycled Paper Greetings, Inc.
3636 North Broadway
Chicago, IL 60613
312-348-6410

◆

Appendix III

SELECTED MAJOR FINE ART POSTER PUBLISHERS AND DISTRIBUTORS

Bruce McGaw Graphics, Inc.
230 Fifth Avenue
New York, NY 10001
212-679-7823

Graphique De France
9 State Street
Woburn, MA 01801
617-935-3405

New York Graphic Society Ltd.
P.O. Box 1469
Greenwich, CT 06836
203-661-2400

◆

Appendix IV

SELECTED IMPORTANT CALENDAR PUBLISHERS

Landmark Calendars
51 Digital Drive
P.O. Box 6105
Novato, CA 94948
415-883-1600

Pomegranate Publications
P.O. Box 808022
Petaluma, CA 94975
800-227-1428; in CA 707-765-2005

Workman Publishing
708 Broadway
New York, NY 10003
800-722-7202

◆

Glossary

Accounts Payable: Money that a business owes.

Accounts Receivable: Money that is owed to a business.

Acquisitions Staff: Those responsible at a publishing company for initiating or acquiring new projects.

Advance: Money paid to an artist or creator as an advance against royalties.

Art: (1) Work product produced by an artist. (2) A phrase used in printing that refers to anything other than text in a reproduction project, for example, photographs, paintings and line art.

Art Poster: See Fine Art Graphic Poster.

Back List: A book publisher's inventory that is not new but is still in print.

Blanket: A fabric coated with rubber which is wrapped around the cylinder of a printing press and serves to transfer ink from plate to paper during the reproduction process.

Break Even Point: The number of copies of a product that must be sold before its costs are made back.

Camera-Ready Material: Mechanicals and artwork that are fully ready to be converted to separations, film and printing plates.

Captive Rack Space: Rack space reserved for the product of a particular publisher.

Captive Rack Space Arrangement: The contractual agreement that reserves rack space for the work of a particular publisher.

Chromalin: Dupont's integral (e.g. one piece) color proofing system.

Chrome: A photographic transparency, also called a slide or a transparency. Chromes are positive, meaning that they appear as the world does, not reversed: blacks are black, and whites are white. See Transparency.

Coated Paper: Paper with a chemical clay-based coating, with either a glossy or a matte finish, which reduces ink absorption.

Color Correction: Improving color rendition of separations by any process, including masking, dot-etching, and digital manipulation of post-scanned computer files.

Color Key: 3M's proprietary color proofing system which uses overlays of colored acetate.

Color Process Printing: A printing technique that first separates and then re-combines process colors of ink to reproduce the full perceived range of colors in artwork. Four-color process, using yellow, cyan, magenta and black, is most commonly used. This color model is also known as "CMYK."

Color Separation: Set of four halftone negatives, one for each of the three primary colors and black, for making plates for color process printing.

Comp: A mock-up that shows what the finished printed piece will look like; often photographic prints are used in place of offset reproductions of imagery.

Comprehensive Dummy: See Comp.

Contact Print: A same-size photo-graphic print.

Continuous Tone: Art which has not been screened and contains smoothly gradient tones.

Copyright: Provides the owner, usually the creator of the work in the absence of a work for hire agreement, with a number of exclusive rights to the copyrighted work. These rights can be summarized as the right to prevent others from exploiting the work for commercial purposes or from using it in a way which prevents the creator from realizing expected profits. Copyrights may be registered with the United States Copyright Office, in which case certain additional presumptions benefit the registrant. Even without registration, however, the creator holds a "common-law" copyright for the work which should be protected by an adequate notice, for example © 1993 Harold Davis.

Crop: To eliminate a portion of a work of art when reproducing it for aesthetic reasons or to fit it into a layout.

Crop Marks: Lines indicating cropping. Usually crop marks are placed on a scaled photostat or photocopier print which is intended for position only.

Deck: A term used in the greeting card industry to describe a stack of greeting cards constituting the entire product line of one manufacturer.

Delivery Memo: A legal document which accompanies a submission of artwork.

Designer: Person responsible for the look, feel, style and format of a product. The designer also creates mechanicals and prepares the art for printing.

Desktop Publishing: Designing publications and setting type using "personal" computers.

Digitize: To convert visual imagery, or other complex analog information, to digital (e.g. binary) form so that it can be manipulated by a computer.

Distributor: A wholesale company that purchases goods from various sources and resells them to the trade.

Display Face: Large size typeface.

Dot Etching: Color correction done by hand on separation film.

Double-Dot Printing: A duotone printing process in which both plates are printed in black. This produces a richer tone than single-dot printing.

DPI: Dots Per Inch.

DTP: See Desktop Publishing.

Dull: A low-gloss, or matte, finish.

Dupe: Duplicate slide.

Duplicate Slide: A transparency that is a copy of another transparency.

Duotone: A two-color halftone reproduction from a monochrome original, requiring two halftone negatives, one for each end of the gray scale. One plate is usually printed in dark ink, the other in a lighter one. A superior form of black & white reproduction.

EIN: Federal Employer Identification Number.

Electronic Retouching: Using a computer to enhance, color correct or alter art that has been scanned.

Encapsulated PostScript File: A computer file of material that has been typeset using the PostScript page description language, and which contains all necessary font resources. A properly created Encapsulated PostScript File is ready to be sent to any service bureau.

.EPS File: See Encapsulated Postscript File.

Exhibition Poster: A poster designed to promote an artist's exhibition at a gallery or museum.

Fake Duotone: A black & white reproduction process that involves placement of a solid tint of color beneath a line-screened halftone that will print in black.

50% of 50: One quarter of the retail price of a product.

Fine Art Graphic Poster: An offset reproduction combining image and graphics designed to be sold as art.

Fine Art Poster: See Fine Art Graphic Poster.

Fine Art Print: See Print.

Flat: In printing, an assembly of negatives stripped together, ready for plate making, and designed to be printed on one sheet.

Float: Accrued interest on money that has been held rather than paid to a supplier.

Font: A complete collection of type of one face containing all its characters; a typeface. For example, Adobe Garamond.

For Position Only: Material used for the sole purpose of showing cropping, positioning and scaling of art; usually a photostat or photocopier print.

Foundation: A not-for-profit organization that is given tax exemption because it gives most of its money away to charitable causes.

Four-Color Process: See Color Process Printing.

FPO: See For Position Only.

Fulfillment: The warehousing, packing and shipping of finished merchandise.

Gloss: Paper, ink or varnish that has a gloss surface and presents the appearance of shining.

Going On Press: Term for client inspection of a printing job as the make-ready progresses.

Halftone: A negative or positive film that results from converting continuous-tone artwork with a screen to an image made up of dots.

Hickey: Small blemish or flaw in printing, usually most visible in areas with heavy ink coverage.

Holding Fee: Charge for holding artwork.

Image Manipulation: Changing the content of imagery, usually via electronic retouching, but sometimes photographically.

Imposition: Arrangement of art and text, as specified in the mechanical, prior to a printing job.

Impression: In printing, one pressing of paper against type, plate or blanket.

In Register: A printing job that is perfectly aligned and appears sharp; see Off Register.

Integral Proof: Proof of color separation negatives exposed in register and appearing on one piece of paper or film.

Inventory: Product, such as cards, calendars or posters, on hand and available for sale.

Invoice: An itemized bill.

Kern: To adjust the space between characters. "Kerning" refers to the way in which inter-character spacing has been adjusted.

Keystone Markup System: A merchandise pricing system under which each entity the product passes through doubles the price.

Layout: A sketch or drawing of a design for a printed piece.

Leading: The amount of space between lines of type, measured from baseline to baseline and expressed in points.

License: The right to use imagery in a specified way.

Limited Edition Print: A fine art print for which the number produced has been strictly limited. Each print should be signed and numbered.

Line Art: Art containing no grays or middle tones that can be reproduced without the use of halftone techniques; for example, a black line around an image.

List: A book publisher's catalog.

Lithography: The generic term for the printing process that uses a chemically treated surface to attract ink to image areas and repels it from non-image areas. See Offset.

Loose Proof: Proof of one color separation.

Make-ready: (1) In printing, the activities required prior to production on a particular project. (2) The paper consumed in this process.

Matchprint: 3M's proprietary integral color proof.

Matte: (1) Slightly dull finish on coated paper stock. (2) Ink or varnish that appears dull when dry.

Mechanical: In printing, camera-ready art consisting of type, graphics and line art showing the exact placement of every element together with for position only reproductions of art and written instructions to the printer. Generally mounted on a board.

Metallic ink: Inks which contain metallic powder mixed with the ink base and appear highly reflective.

Negative: Film that records images in reverse form. Black is white, and white is black.

Net 30 Days: Payment terms on an invoice that means that payment is due thirty days from the invoice date.

Non-Process Colors: Colors that are reproduced without color process separations; spot color.

Off Register: The unsharp appearance of a printing job where perfect register was not achieved; see Register.

Offset: Short for offset lithography,

which is the most common form of lithographic printing. In this process, ink is offset from the plate to a rubber blanket and then to the paper. It is usually the process used when artwork is reproduced in quantity.

Offset Lithography: See Offset.

One-time Rights: The right to reproduce an artwork once for a specified purpose.

Open Edition: An edition of prints or posters whose number has not been limited; not a limited edition.

Pantone Match System: Pantone, Inc.'s proprietary system designed for uniform specification of non-process colors in printing.

Paper Products: Consumer products which are created by printing on paper such as cards, posters and calendars.

Photostat: An inexpensive black & white print used for positioning art.

Plate: A thin sheet of metal that carries the printing image, the surface of which has been treated so that only the desired image is receptive to ink. Separation or other films are used to make plates via a photographic contacting process.

PMS: See Pantone Match System.

Point: A unit of measurement used in typography. There are about seventy-two points to the inch.

Portfolio: A body of work shown by an artist to obtain publication or to solicit assignments or exhibitions.

Positive: A positive appears as the world does, not reversed; blacks are black, and whites are white. See Chrome.

Poster: See Fine Art Graphic Poster.

PostScript: A page description language developed for computers, printers, and high resolution output devices by Adobe Systems, Inc. See Type 1 PostScript.

Press Okay: The approval by the client of a press sheet before the actual production run begins.

Press Proof: Proofs made on a printing press.

Print: A limited edition print, open edition print, poster or reproduction that is intended to be sold as art.

Printer: Person who runs a printing business.

Printing Broker: Agent who supplies printing from various trade vendors for a markup.

Process Printing: See Color Process Printing.

Progressive Proof: Press proof showing each color of a job separately and in progressive combinations.

Proofs: Test materials which are designed to predict how a printing job will come out.

Publisher: Produces and sells (or distributes in some fashion) printed or reproduced material such as cards, posters and calendars.

Quotation: Printer's estimate of the cost of doing a specific job.

Rack Space: Shelf or display space in a store.

Reflected Art: Art, as opposed to transparent art, which is opaque. Examples include photographic prints, paintings, ink on paper, etc. See also Positive; Print.

Register: Accurate alignment of printing plates and paper, necessary to obtain good results.

Rep: See Sales Representative.

Repping Organization: Organization of affiliated independent sales representatives.

Repro Dupe: See Reproduction Duplicate.

Reproduction Duplicate: A duplicate chrome intended for reproduction purposes, generally either 4"X5" or 8"X10".

Retail: (1) Price paid by consumers; the list price. (2) A retail business, such as a card store, that buys from wholesalers and sells to the general public.

Royalty: Often a publisher compensates the creator of a work with a royalty based on a percentage of the retail or wholesale price. Many contracts also provide for a non-refundable advance against royalties.

Sales Representative: An independent manufacturer's representative who sells on a commission basis, generally covering a specific territory with geographic exclusivity.

S.A.S.E.: A self-addressed, stamped, envelope, mandatory when unsolicited submissions are made.

Scaling: The exact percentage enlargement or reduction of art required for it to fit into the design.

Scanner: A scanner is an electronic device that uses laser technology to digitize art.

Screen: A network of crossing lines at regular intervals that, when combined photographically with a continuous tone image, breaks the image up to form a pattern of dots, called a halftone.

Self-Publish: To publish one's own work.

Separation: See Color Separation.

Service Bureau: A company in the business of supplying high resolution output and other graphic art services required by designers.

Sheet-fed Press: A printing press that uses stacks of loose paper as opposed to the continuous roll of paper used by a web press.

Slide: See Chrome.

Sole Proprietorship: A business that is owned by one person and is not a corporation.

Spot Color: Non-process color, usually specified using the Pantone Match System.

Spot Varnish: Varnish applied to a specific portion of a printed sheet, as opposed to an overall application of varnish.

Stat: See Photostat.

Stock Agency: Businesses that maintain libraries of existing artworks in an agency relationship with the artists, primarily photographers, with the intention of licensing the work contained in the library.

Tipping In: Adhering images to backing usually at the corners; for example, attaching photographic prints to greeting card stock.

Trade Printer: A specialty printer who does not generally work with the general public and whose customers are often other printers or printing brokers.

Trade Publication: A publication aimed at businesses in a specialized trade, often not sold to the general public.

Trade Show: A business exposition, convention or fair for a specific industry.

Transparency: Also called a chrome or a slide; a photographic positive viewed by allowing light to pass through it. See Chrome.

Type 1 PostScript: A PostScript font format that has become the de facto standard of designers, service bureaus and the printing industry. See PostScript.

Typeface: A set of characters with design features making them similar to one another and different from all other typefaces, e.g., Adobe Garamond.

Type Family: All styles of a particular typeface, e.g., Adobe Garamond, Adobe Garamond Italic, Adobe Garamond Expert, Adobe Garamond Bold, etc.

Typography: (1) The design of printed pieces using type. (2) Setting type.

Uncoated Paper: Paper on which the printing surface consists of the stock itself.

Unit Cost: What it costs to produce each unit of a product.

Varnish: A thin, protective coating applied to a printed sheet on press for beauty and protection. Varnish is either gloss or dull. It can be applied to part of a printed piece (see Spot Varnish) or overall.

Vendor: A supplier.

Wholesale: The price at which a product is sold to a store.

Wholesaler: A company that is in the business of distributing at wholesale to the trade.

Work For Hire: A relationship in which all rights, title, and interest in a creative work, including the copyright, is owned by the commissioning party, and not by the creator. ◆

Index

About the Author

Harold Davis is an author, business consultant, photographer and publisher. He is the President of Wilderness Studio, Inc. and the creator of many well-known fine art posters. His photographs are widely exhibited, collected and published. He is the author of the *Photographer's Publishing Handbook* and *Successful Fine Art Photography*. Mr. Davis holds degrees in Computer Science and Law. He lives in New York City with his wife, Phyllis, who designed this book. ◆